# THE ULTIMATE HOLISTIC HANDBOOK FOR BEGINNERS

# Healing Like Nature Intended

**EMBRACING A HOLISTIC LIFESTYLE** begins with knowing that you already have the tools to find peace of mind—you just need to learn how to access them. From staying hydrated to eating whole foods to walking in the sunshine, your journey to vitality starts by reframing your daily habits. Learn the secrets to keeping your stress in check, increasing your flexibility through simple stretches and healing your body with a garden full of remedies you can grow in your own backyard. The *Holistic Handbook* will help you recharge your mind, body and soul with tips on how to find balance in all aspects of your life. Your journey to a more centered self starts here.

## 05
# Mindfulness
Finding Your Moment of Zen Every Day

## 21
# Nutrition
Eating Your Way to a Healthier Life

## 45
# Fitness
Power Poses to Keep You on the Go

## 69
# Happier You
Tips to Amp Up Your Serotonin Intake

## 83
### SPECIAL SECTION
# Nature's Remedies
Your Herbal Index of Nature's Remedies

# Mindfulness

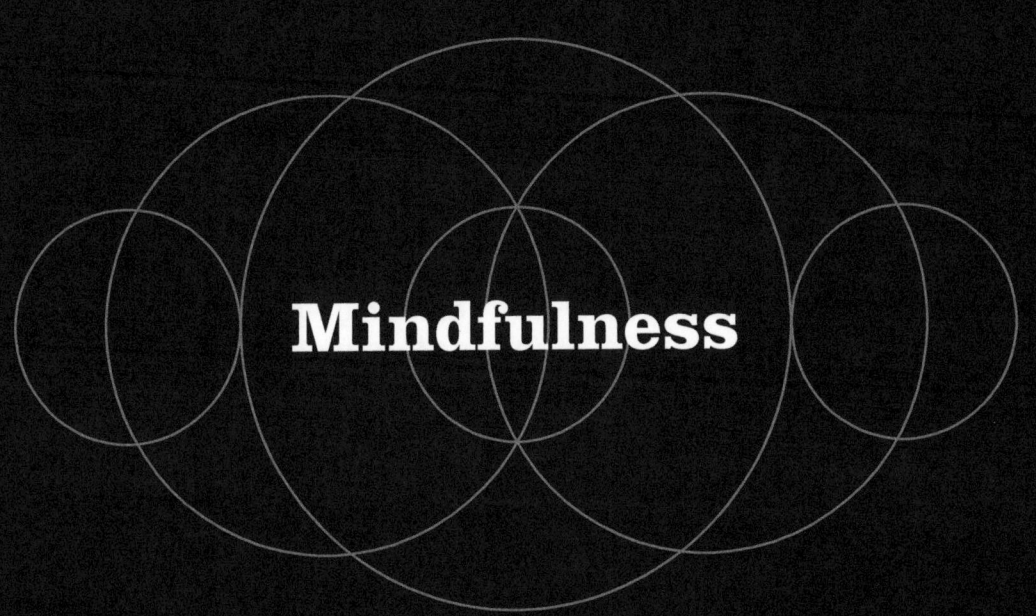

Find your center. Take a breath. Approach your day with intention. These are the techniques that will help you transcend the grind.

MINDFULNESS

# Visualizing Peace and Touching Quiet

For author and instructor Kristin McGee's overstressed students, mindfulness is—miraculously—just a few thoughts and a breath or two away.

IMAGINE YOUR MIND as a pristine lake. It can be a desert oasis beset with leaning palms, a simple backyard pond or a mountaintop expanse surrounded by nothing but stone and clouds—whatever enclosed body of water presents the most pleasing image for you. Now imagine that pebbles begin falling into the water. There are only a few at first, but before long there is a monsoon of pebbles of various sizes assaulting the lake.

If each pebble represents a thought, idea or stress stimulus hitting the calm surface of the lake that is your mind during the course of a day, imagine the ripples as their cumulative effect on your psyche. Each phone alert, headline, commercial, inbox ping and appointment pelt the surface, creating violent splashes where still water once sat.

Now follow the pebbles beneath the surface and down to the lake's bottom. Imagine them coming to rest with the curious grace small objects have when falling through liquid—tiny inanimate cranes coming to rest after effortless flybys. Now look up and notice that as the pebbles fell, while you were invested in the moment of their transit, the lake became still again.

This visualization exercise, outlined for *Newsweek* by Kristin McGee, author of *Chair Yoga* and a New York-based instructor of both yoga and pilates, amounts to a free lesson from one of the most sought-after mindfulness experts in the U.S. And according to McGee, helping her students become present and mindful—focused completely on the moment at hand—is just as important as their physical progress. Some, she says, feel most able to achieve such a mindful state through visualization exercises.

When I point out that the best jump shooters in basketball and shot-makers in golf necessarily describe an uncanny level of acuity in such exercises, she agrees and also counters by stating that brilliant dancers have been known to feel the same calm focus as Dustin Johnson visualizing a long putt by focusing on tactile contact with the ground or of their dance partner. "How a person connects with the moment they're in varies based on the personality." For this reason, McGee's technique combines visualization with more tactile exercises. "The first thing I tell my students to do is to notice where they're making contact," says McGee. "If they're seated, they're making contact with the floor through their sit bones and feeling themselves anchored into the floor. I think of the sit bones as a two-pronged plug and the floor as a socket. The second someone roots down and feels connected it's like shaking someone's hand or making eye contact—presence is gained."

And for McGee, setting aside the worries and stimuli of the past and present in favor of total presence is the first step in making the jump to a more mindful state—a state McGee says makes her students more confident, calm and centered when it can be reached at will. "I always say no matter what you're doing, first you make contact," she continues. "Whether you're meeting with someone or just sitting down, you make contact in order to be present: Make contact with your feet on the ground or with your back if you're lying down. The process forces you to engage and be present before you deal with the more subtle body through breathing exercises."

When coupled with the kind of presence McGee's students strive to achieve, simple breathing exercises can often be the final piece of the puzzle for those hoping to think themselves into a calmer, more present state. "I tell students to focus by counting their breath or paying attention to where the breath is going in your body," she says. "I also have them slow their breathing down on the exhale. Oftentimes we don't fully exhale before taking another breath, but we want to be completely empty before we focus on filling the entire body again." Breath control of this kind is common for those who practice yoga or martial arts, but coupled with McGee's ideas form a new mindfulness template.

Most of all, McGee stresses that this kind of simple visualization, presence and breathing, though it doesn't fit the textbook definition of formal meditation, is just that: meditation. "I'm a new mom, and my students who have young children often say, 'I don't have time to meditate.'" But McGee doesn't buy the excuse, taking the stance that meditation is more than its stereotypes. "I always say they should meditate while they're with their kids. When they're playing, really be present with that toy. When they're reading a book [to their child], really be mindful of every aspect of the book as you read aloud. People tend to think of meditation in its formal state, but you can meditate in any moment as long as you're present in that moment."

Teaching the Big Apple's elite workaholics, worry warts and power parents how to take it easy for a few minutes might be a labor worthy of Greek myth, but for McGee, mindfulness is a goal everyone—most of all the "Type-A New Yorkers" she says make up her student body—can benefit from achieving. "Running around and distracted" is how she describes the default settings of many of her adepts—and it doesn't seem like a stretch for most of the modern American population to see themselves fitting a similar description. The good news is that for the mindful, respite is just a few breaths and a thought or two away.

MINDFULNESS

# A Short History of Zen

Achieving enlightenment through Zen has a 1,500-year-long backstory.

ZEN IS FREQUENTLY tossed around as a word interchangeable with tranquility, serenity and peace. While the associated words may seem simplistic, the history of Zen is much more storied and complex. In famed Zen Master D. T. Suzuki's book *An Introduction to Zen Buddhism*, he explains that there's no singular definition of Zen, but it can be described as "the finger pointing at the moon." The moon—awakening, enlightenment, understanding and insight; the finger—Zen teachings covering a cross-section of schools that implement various forms of meditation, self-control, breath observation and scripture.

Originating as "Chan" Buddhism during the Tang Dynasty (7th to 10th century) in China, Zen is an even more introspective version of Mahayana Buddhism. While theories about the early formation of Chan vary, many scholars believe it developed when Buddhism was exposed to Taoist practices in China. Taoism was the dominating philosophical tradition in China at the time—the main doctrines, or the Three Treasures of which were compassion, frugality and humility. With traditional Buddhism blending with Taoist meditation, Chan became a "natural evolution" of the two, according to Suzuki.

The teachings of a Taoist adept, Bodhidharma, which were introduced in the 6th century, wouldn't gain prominence for another two centuries. His teachings extended on traditional Buddhist thought by focusing on acceptance of suffering by way of meditation and self-control. Bodhidharma is considered the First Patriarch of Chan, and he began a lineage of influential successors who would continue expanding on these disciplines. By the time the Fourth Patriarch, Daoxin, was Master, Chan had begun taking shape as a distinct school with a dedicated congregation. The school finally found its stride in the year 700 when they were invited to the Imperial Court by Empress Wu—earning Chan their long sought-after stamp of legitimacy.

More and more schools of Chan began popping up as the practice became accessible and accepted. Chan was on an upswing until 845, when Emperor Wuzong persecuted and destroyed most Buddhist schools in China. While he claimed they were a drain on the economy, he was actually just a dedicated Taoist who thought Buddhist influence was harmful to Chinese society. Not many schools survived, but those that did developed into the Five "Houses" of Chan—Guiyang, Linji, Caodong, Fayan and Yunmen. Together, they worked to make Chan the dominant stream of Buddhism in China and had succeeded after this persecution. The Linji and Caodong schools became the most powerful, and they both began spreading their teachings to Vietnam, Korea and Japan. It was the Japanese pronunciation of Chan—Zen—that emerged as the mainstream title of this school of thought.

When Soyen Shaku (pictured) appeared among the first speakers at the Columbian Exposition's religion summit in 1893, he and his fellow dignitaries inaugurated a tradition of dialogue among faiths that was eventually revived, with seven "World Parliament of Religions" gatherings taking place since the 100th anniversary of Shaku's debut in 1993.

# Mind Over Stressors

How a mindfulness regimen can improve your health and even help mitigate illness symptoms.

ACCORDING TO Dr. Saki Santorelli, Professor of Medicine at UMass Medical School and director of the university's Mindfulness-Based Stress Reduction Clinic (MBSR), not only are oft-repeated myths about stress affecting your physical health true, but a background in mindfulness can actually help offset these effects. The MBSR program, which hopes to synchronize medicine and mindfulness, allowing both to inform our medical future, has been integral to the university's understanding of the relationship between stress and mindfulness since 1979. It has recently begun connecting people from all over the world with the school's mindfulness teachers, and approaches mindfulness holistically, regardless of whether they can ever set foot on the UMass campus. Santorelli even points out that after one year of exposure to mindfulness techniques, visits to primary care physicians, emergency rooms and hospitals were all decreased observably.

**ASTHMA**
In the 2012 study "Effect of Mindfulness Training on Quality of Life and Lung Function: A Randomized Controlled Trial," the conclusion was drawn that "MBSR produced lasting clinically significant improvements in asthma-related quality of

It's difficult to pinpoint exactly when Zen entered the Western world. American interest in Zen is usually attributed to Japanese Zen monk Soyen Shaku, who visited the Columbian Exhibition at Chicago in 1893. He participated in the World Parliament of Religions and presented a speech entitled "The Law of Cause and Effect, as Taught By Buddha." He brought his English-speaking student, D. T. Suzuki, to translate. Suzuki ended up staying in Illinois to write multiple books on Zen including 1914's *An Introduction to Zen Buddhism*. His teachings were instrumental in the spreading of Zen in the West, as he modernized the philosophy for Western audiences. As more monks immigrated to the United States in the 20th century, Zen became a key influence to high-profile thinkers such as Carl Jung, Jack Kerouac and Alan Watts.

# MINDFULNESS

life and stress in patients with persistent asthma, even in the absence of improvements in lung function," according to Santorelli. But the most impressive thing about this proven boon for asthmatics is that an even bigger study is currently underway hoping to cement the finding even further.

### ANXIETY DISORDER
In another controlled experiment hoping to prove MBSR's effectiveness at mitigating everyday illnesses, patients with general anxiety disorder were exposed to MBSR and, compared to the control group, showed significantly larger reductions in stress hormones and inflammatory responses to stress.

### STOMACH ISSUES
Citing the largest ever study involving Irritable Bowel Syndrome and MBSR, Dr. Santorelli claims the program proved to be an effective way to treat symptom severity of IBS as well as an effective way to maintain those changes. Though stress has not been proven to cause irritable bowel syndrome, it can exacerbate the condition, making mindfulness a powerful tool for sufferers.

# Debunking Stress Myths

**We all know it's a killer, but many of us think we know more than we do.**

### Are major physical problems the best indicators of chronic stress?

Stress can eventually manifest in many serious and threatening ways—including stroke, insomnia, heart palpitations and weight gain. But just because you aren't experiencing any of these problems doesn't mean that stress isn't taking a toll on you. Stress is often known as the "silent killer" because people don't take it seriously until it causes a serious issue. If you're stressed and think you don't have symptoms, there's a good chance it's still affecting your body. Chronic high-stress lifestyles can cause a buildup of symptoms not immediately associated with stress such as, migraines, changes in sex drive, muscle aches and even a weakened immune system, according to the Mayo Clinic.

### Isn't a little bit of stress a good thing?

Stress, whether it be before a big exam or important work presentation, is often viewed as something that motivates us to work harder. Many carry the belief that being stressed pushes a greater desire to succeed—and therefore stress creates positive action. However, Andrew Bernstein, author of *The Myth of Stress*, argues that the motivation to work harder actually arises from stimulation and engagement. He uses the example of goal setting as a proper motivator. The goal of wanting to succeed keeps us engaged and energetic, while stress is just a negative and impending emotion. Bernstein believes, "If you're successful and stressed out, you're succeeding in spite of your stress, not because of it."

### If I have a drink (or two) after a stressful day, will it help to unwind?

It's not uncommon to reach for a bottle at the end of a long day or week. But surprisingly, indulging in a few drinks to destress isn't working in your favor. A 2008 study published in the *Journal of Clinical Endocrinology & Metabolism* indicated that cortisol, a stress hormone, is actually released when alcohol is consumed. Instead of alleviating stress, alcohol only triggers it further. While our body self regulates cortisol by way of the hypothalamus, excessive exposure to the hormone can cause depression and anxiety disorders, weight gain and hair loss.

### Aren't stress and anxiety just different words for the same thing?

Though it's pretty normal to hear these words used interchangeably, medically there is a very important distinction between stress and anxiety. Stress is a reaction to a specific stimulus or situation, known as a stressor. When the stressor is no longer a factor—when you meet the deadline, escape the danger or achieve your goal—the stress disappears. Anxiety is a condition wherein, despite the fact that the stressors are no longer immediate, stress continues.

MINDFULNESS

# Natural Depression Remedies

Those suffering from clinical depression might consider these solutions as part of their overall regimen.

AS OF 2015, about 16.1 million adults in the U.S. had experienced at least one major depressive episode in the past year, according to the Anxiety and Depression Association of America. Those who suffer from depression feel chronic sadness, hopelessness or lack of motivation enough to interfere with basic routine and societal functions. While prescription medications can be an important part of treating symptoms of depression, there are also natural activities that can complement medication and help battle depression to improve quality of life.

### EXERCISE
Studies have shown activity can help combat depression and that a lack of exercise can increase the risks of a slump. Exercise releases endorphins, which serve as a natural antidepressant. It can also improve your mood by releasing other neurotransmitters such as serotonin, a lack of which can directly lead to depression.

### B VITAMINS
B-12, the B vitamin most closely associated with mood regulation, is found (in large quantities) in fish, lean meat, poultry, eggs and low-fat and fat-free milk. Fortified cereals also tend to contain plenty of B vitamins. Eating a diet rich in B vitamins might help alleviate depression symptoms.

### WELL-BALANCED DIET
If your diet is balanced and natural, it will provide all the various proteins, vitamins and acids the human body needs. Studies completed in Spain and the U.K. have shown that a diet high in vegetables, fruits, fish, nuts, whole grains and olive oil could help with depression. Foods like chicken, turkey and beans that are high in tryptophan, an amino acid that is converted into serotonin, can also be helpful.

### MOOD-ENHANCING SUPPLEMENTS
Taking a pill for depression doesn't necessarily mean taking something synthetic. Dietary and herbal supplements and natural herbs such as St. John's wort, SAMe, fish oil, L-Theanine and 5-HTP are popular for fighting depression.

### MEDITATION
According to some studies, meditation can help fight anxiety, depression and pain. Mindfulness

> ## CAFFEINE?
> Caffeine can provide a short boost, but when its effects end, it causes a crash. It also might interfere with regular moods. Drinking too much caffeine can cause shakiness or anxiety and might actually worsen depression symptoms in those who suffer chronically, so it's best to consume in moderation, if at all.

meditation's purpose is to make the brain stay in the moment; participants are supposed to let go of regrets and anxiety. It's also free and has no harmful side effects.

### SUNLIGHT/LIGHT THERAPY
Spending some time in the sun increases the brain's serotonin levels, which can improve your mood. Soaking up some rays can work more quickly than prescribed medication and has fewer side effects (though you should always take care to protect yourself from UV rays). Light therapy is often used to treat the type of depression called seasonal affective disorder and can help regularize moods.

# Mood-Boosting Magnets

## A new alternative to conventional treatments for depression.

ONE OF THE LEADING causes of disability in the United States isn't physical—it's mental. According to the Anxiety and Depression Association of America (ADAA), 15 million adults—approximately 6.7 percent of the population—suffer from major depressive disorder, which is most often treated through a combination of talk therapy and medication. Those who struggle with depression have imbalanced levels of serotonin, which maintains mood, and dopamine, which controls the pleasure and reward zones. The brain's synapses control how much of these chemicals are released, and drugs like Zoloft effectively prevent the little serotonin being produced from reabsorbing back into the nerve cells from which they were released, resulting in a higher concentration of serotonin. Some pill-averse patients have longed for a natural cure for depression, while others complain that the drugs they're on aren't enough. Hope for both groups may have arrived through an unlikely source: magnets. Researchers discovered they can harness the power of magnetism to increase serotonin production and combat depression through a process called Transcranial Magnetic Stimulation (TMS).

"Each [symptom of depression] maps onto a given circuit of the brain," neurologist Alvaro Pascual-Leone told NPR in April 2016 about treating patients using TMS. "The reason why that circuit of the brain is not functioning properly...has to do with a deficit of a certain chemical in the brain. But the point is that if we can identify the circuit that causes the symptoms, we can target that circuit and make it function better through brain stimulation. So, in a sense, [TMS is] not a treatment...for the ultimate cause of the disorder, but it's an intervention that improves how the patient is able to function."

TMS has a lot in common with a traditional MRI scan. In fact, the only clue TMS treatment contains magnets at all is that patients must remove any jewelry and stow their credit cards (to prevent demagnetization) before treatment. According to Johns Hopkins University School of Medicine's description of the technique, a coil is fitted to the front of a patient's head so the electromagnetic pulses can target the prefrontal cortex of the brain, which controls emotion. A physician then tests the machine to see how much power is needed to affect the patient's reflexes. Once the patient's thumb involuntarily twitches, the current is strong enough to affect the patient's brain activity. At this point, specific symptoms can be targeted depending on the patient's needs.

The biggest drawback to TMS, according to advocates, is the limitations on just who can undergo the treatment. Though it was approved by the FDA in 2008, its use is federally restricted with exemptions only for those with severe depression, autism or Parkinson's. Even those who are approved to undergo the treatment face another barrier as TMS is not widely covered by health insurance.

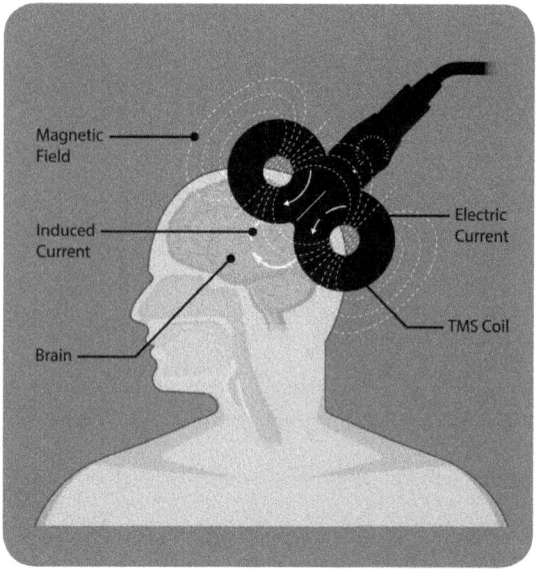

An image of a Transcranial Magnetic Stimulation at work. Although the cost of TMS therapy varies with each patient, a person can expect to pay between $6,000 and $12,000 for a full course of therapy.

Its efficacy varies from patient to patient and, like most prescriptions for depression, TMS has its own set of side-effects. The most common, not surprisingly, are headaches. Although one-third of patients have reported experiencing painful scalp sensations and facial twitching, these tend to fade after several treatments.

Despite these setbacks, researchers are optimistic about TMS—and not just as a form of treatment for depression. Experiments treating Parkinson's and autism, the other two conditions for which TMS is approved, have seen some success among neurologists. More studies will be needed to determine whether this method can be used as a widespread treatment for other brain-related disorders, but if today's research is any indication, TMS could be a key to improving the lives of Americans suffering from a multitude of disorders.

# Your Work Stress Checklist

It's No. 1 with a bullet on most of our stressor lists, but dealing with work is easier than it seems.

According to the American Institute of Stress, 46 percent of workplace stress has to do with sheer workload, followed by "People Issues" at 28 percent, lack of work-life balance at 20 percent and lack of job security at 6 percent.

**E**VERYONE COPES with the responsibilities and stresses of the adult world differently, but we all experience them. No one can promise to take the stress entirely out of the office, but being mindful of the world beyond the cubicle as well as the world between one's ears can be a great start toward focus and acceptance. Your ideal work-life balance might take some time to perfect, but this simple checklist will help you identify exactly what possible changes in your routine might help to de-stress the workday.

○ *Are there any immediate changes to thermal comfort, lighting, etc. that could make you more comfortable at work?*
○ *When was the last time you spoke openly and honestly with superiors about your workplace concerns?*
○ *Are you allowing personal stress, whether financial, romantic or otherwise, to affect your demeanor or productivity?*
○ *Are you being realistic when taking on new responsibilities? Do you feel that you can say no?*
○ *Are you flexible when necessary but stand your ground when the time is right, or do you sometimes argue for argument's sake?*
○ *When was the last time you took a day off to indulge your hobbies or interests?*
○ *Do you have trouble sharing your burdens or asking for help?*
○ *Have you and other members of your workforce discussed the stress levels in the office? Are you alone in feeling over-stressed?*
○ *Has your employer explored policies and programs regarding stress minimization?*

MINDFULNESS

# Your Happier Sleep Checklist

**Better shut-eye is something all mindfulness experts agree can help with focus, energy, contentedness and health.**

The National Institute of Health estimates 30 percent of American adults have suffered some form of sleep disruption.

HARDLY A doctor's visit goes by without every American hearing the following sentence in one form or another: "You really should be trying to get between eight and 10 hours of sleep a night." And most of us then roll our eyes wondering who these modern anomalies who sleep 10 hours a night are. While the following checklist won't change your schedule for you, it might make the sleep you do get a lot more satisfying.

- *Cut down on the amount of caffeine you consume in a day and try not to have any caffeine after 5 p.m.*
- *Set aside 10 or 15 minutes during the day to write down everything that's worrying you—if you engage during the day, it can keep these worries from entering your mind once your head hits the pillow.*
- *Try to stop using all screen-based devices a half-hour before turning in—the bright lights can affect your eyes for long periods of time.*
- *Do your best to control the temperature of your bedroom—fluctuations can disturb sleep.*
- *Use progressive muscle relaxation, individually tightening and releasing muscles from your feet up to your shoulders and neck, after laying down.*
- *Try to eat your last meal more than 3 hours before bed.*
- *If you can't sleep, don't stay in bed, get up and perform a relaxing or repetitive task for a few minutes.*

# Your Happy Checklist

Finding your happy place is more than just a cliché: It's an exercise that can de-stress you in moments.

Fresh air is often a key part of calming because oxygen gives natural energy without the side effects of caffeine.

ONE PRACTICE that it seems all mindfulness experts can agree on is visualization. By concentrating hard on an image or memory, the human mind can actually overcome the stresses surrounding it. The technique is practiced by more non-experts than you might think and has a relatively colloquial name: Finding a "Happy Place." The human mind is a marvel of evolution, but it can be fooled into thinking an intense visualization is real, allowing such a "place" to be accessed. All this cliché really means is, "Be present in a moment and content with that presence." Using this simple checklist, you can achieve mindfulness and inhabit your own "Happy Place."

- *Are your surroundings as free of stress and physically relaxing to you as possible?*
- *Are you sitting, standing or lying down comfortably?*
- *Can you recall a particularly happy memory?*
- *Can you call to mind as many details of this memory as possible?*
- *Have you relaxed your muscles?*
- *Have you relaxed your body to the best of your ability?*
- *Can you visualize yourself actually inhabiting your memory?*
- *Have you incorporated the memories of all five senses?*

THE ULTIMATE HOLISTIC HANDBOOK FOR BEGINNERS 17

MINDFULNESS

# Your Big Decision Checklist

Before making a life-changing decision, cut down on stress by asking yourself these simple questions.

**Indecision, closely linked to both depression and anxiety, can become chronic in some individuals.**

**M**AKING DECISIONS with large consequences—buying a home or car, proposing to a significant other, accepting a new job that requires a cross-country move—can be among the most stressful events that don't actually involve life or death in some form. Indecision can be such a stressful feeling that even smaller choices, like where to take that long-saved-for vacation or what to get a loved one for their birthday, can seem bigger than they really are. But these simple questions, meant to help you arrive at an objective and mindful decision, can make all the difference.

○ *Have I "fallen in love" with one of these ideas against my better judgment?*
○ *Have I asked myself the questions about this decision I do not necessarily want to hear?*
○ *Have I looked for a dissenting opinion?*
○ *If I had a year to decide, what would I want to know?*
○ *Am I making any false comparisons? (For example, are you assuming success based on a past success, as in, "They say it's very nice in _____ this time of year.")*
○ *Is a fear of change guiding my decision?*
○ *What are the best- and worst-case scenarios for each option?*

# Notes

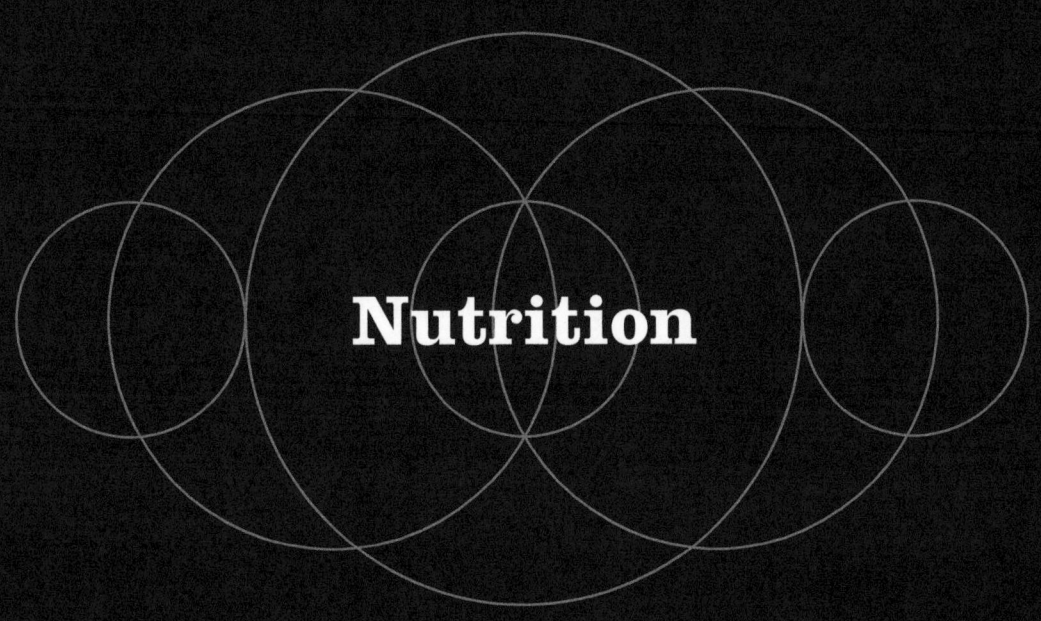

# Nutrition

You are what you eat is as clichéd as it is accurate. Learn more about the value of quality ingredients here.

# Comfort Foods

Relax and unwind with these 10 superfoods.

**1 DARK CHOCOLATE**
The best excuse to indulge in this treat is that it's a surefire stress reliever. Rich in antioxidants, dark chocolate relaxes the walls of your blood vessels, which in turn lowers blood pressure and enhances circulation. It also reduces stress hormones such as cortisol and catecholamines, and if that isn't enough, dark chocolate is also known to release endorphins in your brain

**2 LEAFY GREENS**
Green leafy veggies such as kale, collard greens, Swiss chard and spinach are packed with folate. The benefits of folate (vitamin B9) are seemingly endless—promoting colon, heart and neural health are just a few examples. Folate is also useful for mood management. It helps the body manufacture and absorb neurotransmitters such as dopamine and serotonin, which regulate mood.

**3 MILK**
The childhood tradition of drinking warm milk before bed brings back memories of comfort for a reason. Milk releases an essential amino acid called tryptophan, which helps decrease stress. Milk is also high in vitamin D which positively affects serotonin production. When serotonin levels are running low, you're more likely to be anxious, irritable and stressed—so a glass of milk before bed is perfect for winding down.

**4 OATMEAL**
All carbs release serotonin in the body, but complex carbs provide the best supply of this feel-good chemical. Because they take longer to digest, we feel the effects of complex carbs like pasta, whole-grain bread and cereal for a greater amount of time. Oatmeal is an especially effective complex carb because of its high levels of potassium and magnesium, which lower blood pressure

**5 CARROTS**
Whenever you're stressed or anxious, much of that tension gets stored in the jaw. Munching on raw veggies like carrots releases the tension you're holding in your face, and is a healthier alternative to stress-chomping on sugary gum.

**6 CHAMOMILE TEA**
There's evidence to back up chamomile's longtime claim of being a bedtime soother. A study at the University of Pennsylvania gave chamomile supplements to participants with generalized anxiety disorder. After the eight-week study, the participants found they had a significant drop in anxiety symptoms. Whether you like drinking your chamomile or you prefer it in capsule form, the herb relaxes muscles and has a sedative effect on the central nervous system.

**7 SALMON**
Fatty fish such as salmon and tuna have high levels of DHA, an omega-3 fatty acid. Omega-3s produce antioxidants and detoxification enzymes that work against high levels of stress. A pilot study done by Massachusetts General Hospital's Center for Women's Mental Health also suggests that these fatty acids work well to decrease levels of stress during pregnancy.

**8 BLUEBERRIES**
This superfruit packs tons of health properties into a tiny shell, all due to its high levels of anthocyanin, a type of antioxidant. Anthocyanin boosts cognitive function, reduces risk of heart disease and lowers cholesterol. Blueberries

# The "Superfood" Question

**Separating truth from hype can be difficult, but some foods really can be super.**

THERE'S BEEN a lot of marketing centered around so-called "superfoods" in the past, and it should come as no surprise that research has proven some foods are much less deserving of the word super than their pitchmen would have you believe. But that doesn't mean there aren't foods packing more than their share of nutrients into a package that puts minimal strain on your body. And when it comes down to it, getting more than you put in is a dream for anyone trying to live a healthy lifestyle. In an informative conversation with the American Heart Association, dietician Penny Kris-Etherton, Ph.D., RD, said that so-called "superfoods" can really have tangible health benefits if incorporated into a generally healthy diet. What these foods can do, according to Kris-Etherton, is focus the benefits of a healthy diet on specific issues.

## STRESS

A 2001 study helped begin the superfood craze by encouraging people to think outside the box when looking for the possible health benefits of food. Seeking to find a correlation between vitamin C intake and levels of psychological stress, the study, published in

---

are also rich in vitamin C, which is helpful in combating anxiety by managing the levels of stress hormone cortisol.

### 9 GARLIC

Garlic contains allicin, a compound that's been linked to fending off everything from the common cold to heart disease. Because high-stress lifestyles take a heavy toll on the immune system, including a little extra garlic in your meal is a great way to toughen up your immunity.

### 10 AVOCADOS

Low levels of potassium lead to a greater risk of mood disturbances, irritability, depression and tension. This is because potassium ensures the brain's ability to produce and properly utilize serotonin. While you can always reach for a banana, avocados are also a great alternative. Half an avocado contains more potassium than a whole banana!

THE ULTIMATE HOLISTIC HANDBOOK FOR BEGINNERS

# NUTRITION

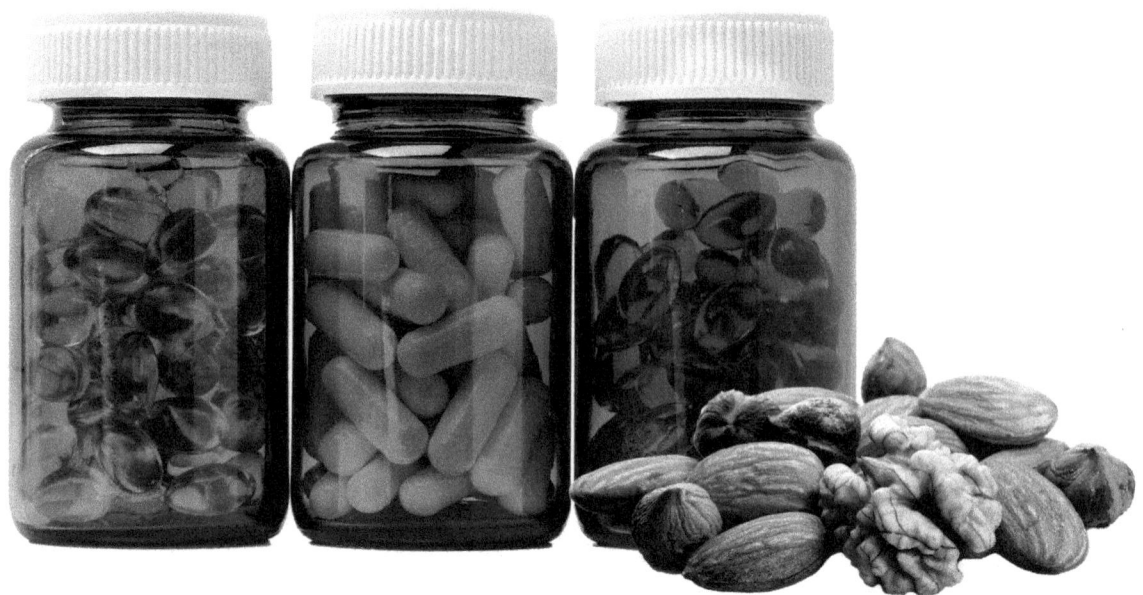

the journal *Psychopharmacology*, found that stress hormone levels were diminished for 60 adults who'd been dosed with vitamin C for two weeks. While more serious anxiety might call for heavy-duty remedies, a quick break for some ascorbic acid-rich fruits such as blueberries does seem to decrease stress.

## HEART HEALTH

According to the American Heart Association, there are plenty of fruits, vegetables, nuts and seeds like berries, gourds and kernels that are rich in phytochemicals—compounds found exclusively in plants—that studies have shown could help reduce the risk of atherosclerosis, a condition where fatty buildup masses on artery walls. But the AHA also cautions against ingesting these superfoods prepared in ways that add sugar and calories, (such as almonds covered in milk chocolate) which can erase any health benefits.

## DENTAL HEALTH

A 2015 study done by Contemporary Clinical Dentistry sought to determine whether a superfood-based remedy, green tea mouthwash, would be able to replace traditional mouthwash without subjecting consumers to the same side effects. Not only did the study conclude that green tea mouthwash was just as effective as an antibacterial such as traditional mouthwash, but it also offers the opportunity to save money by making the mouthwash at home.

## CELLULAR HEALTH

According to the U.K.'s National Health Service, free radicals are naturally occurring particles in humans that are thought to cause cell damage. Antioxidants are some of the most touted superfood components because they can help neutralize those free radicals and keep our cells—and by extension our organs—functioning at their best. Fish and food rich in vitamins A, C and E are particular examples, but as the AHA says, the manner of preparation can determine exactly how pronounced the benefits can be.

# Naturally Slimming

Science has shown these six foods and supplements can help shed pounds.

**T**HERE'S NO getting around it: In order to lose fat, people need to burn more calories than they take in. And while there's no such thing as a pill that will allow a person to eat as much as they want and still lose weight, there are some foods and supplements that can help kick your weight loss plan into high gear.

### GREEN TEA
Green tea contains an ingredient called EGCG (epigallocatechin gallate), which is thought to have numerous health benefits, including lowering the risk of cancer. In order to determine whether EGCG has any effect on weight loss, researchers at Anglia Ruskin University conducted a study on the effects of decaffeinated green tea combined with cycling. The study suggests that combined with exercise, green tea can help people lose weight more efficiently: Those who took green tea capsules reduced body fat by 1.63 percent more than the control group. If you're looking to use green tea to boost weight loss, consider ingesting it in pill form—it would take six to seven cups of tea daily to get the required dosage of EGCG.

### COFFEE
Studies have shown that caffeine, ingested in the form of coffee, can slightly increase your

**Americans who drink java down an average of 3.2 cups of coffee each day.**

metabolic rate for a few hours. Caffeine is also known to enhance energy and alertness, meaning you may be a bit more active after a cup of joe. Additionally, choosing a cup of coffee to boost your energy results in ingesting far fewer calories than, say, a granola bar. However, in order to maximize the weight-loss benefits of coffee, make sure to drink it black: The calories in cream or sugar will likely negate or even exceed any extra calories you burn off.

### PROBIOTICS
If you're wondering why products like kombucha are popping up everywhere, the answer may have something to do with probiotics. Probiotics are live bacteria (the good kind) that can help regulate the bacteria in your gut. Researchers have found evidence to support the theory that probiotics can help counteract obesity and

# NUTRITION

Losing weight is about more than just vanity. According to a meta-analysis published in the *Journal of the American Medical Association* of 100 studies on body mass and mortality, those with a body mass index of 35 or greater were associated with "significantly higher all-cause mortality."

even diabetes, and they are beneficial in the treatment and prevention of gastrointestinal diseases. If you're not into kombucha, yogurt, sauerkraut and miso soup all pack a healthy dose of probiotics.

## GLUCOMANNAN

Glucomannan is a weight-loss pill that actually works! It's a supplement of dietary fiber that comes from the roots of the konjac plant. Because glucomannan takes up space in the stomach and delays it from emptying, it works well as an appetite suppressant. A diet high in fiber is also shown to reduce the absorption of protein and fat. Aside from taking glucomannan, it's generally wise to choose foods that are naturally high in fiber, like whole grains, berries, split peas, beans and lentils.

## COCONUT OIL

People use coconut oil as a moisturizer, wood polish, insect repellent and more, and now there's science to support its use for weight loss. Coconut oil is fatty, but not all fats are created equal. It's is high in fats called medium-chain triglycerides, which have been shown to increase metabolism and help people eat fewer calories. Because coconut oil is still high in calories, it's best to use it sparingly and in place of (not in addition to) other cooking oils and butter.

## CAPSAICIN

Scientists have discovered that capsaicin burns more than just your tongue—it's responsible for helping burn fat, too. Known as the component that gives chili peppers their spice, researchers have determined capsaicin is effective in reducing energy and fat intake, as well as increasing satiety. If you can't handle the heat, there's still good news: Studies have also shown the capsiate found in sweet peppers can also increase energy and boost fat oxidation.

# Alternatives to Cleansing

Detoxifying cleanses have gained popularity and even celebrity converts, but are they really all that miraculous?

While people who adhere to a cleanse can see the number on the scale drop, the extremely low caloric intake makes it difficult to safely exercise, which provides a whole host of physical and mental benefits.

PROPONENTS OF cleansing say that just by limiting your food and drink intake to a specified minimum, you can detoxify your body and achieve a number of general health goals from better mental acuity to more regular bowel movements and everything in between. But no matter how prevalent cleanses have become, as of press time no studies have been able to conclusively say that cleansing does in fact help your overall health. More importantly, cleansing can have a negative impact—by not eating all day, you can feel light-headed and nauseated. Certain cleanses forbid exercise, which seems counterintuitive to those who are hoping to achieve overall wellness. Instead of opting for extreme methods that might offer short-term results, focus on long-term solutions that can dramatically change your life—or at least your health—for the better.

### WANT TO LOSE WEIGHT?
*Skip the Master Cleanse and monitor your caloric intake instead.*
One of the most popular cleanses, the Master Cleanse, requires ingesting nothing but a concoction of lemon juice, maple syrup, cayenne pepper and water for 10 days or more. If that doesn't sell you, know in advance that taking laxatives is also a vital part to losing

# NUTRITION

those 10 pounds and "feeling great." The cleanse can cause dramatic weight-loss in the short term, but it's only a temporary victory. Those pounds you're losing aren't excess fat. They're just water weight. When you dramatically decrease how many calories you consume, your body uses its stores of glycogen, which live in your muscles and liver. Glycogen binds itself to water, so when your body loses its stores, the water is released and so is a percentage of your overall mass.

This immediate result is both the reason why the Master Cleanse became so popular and the reason it's so flawed. You'll gain all those pounds back once your cleanse is over and you start eating regular food again. A much more sustainable weight-loss program involves tracking your calorie intake (you can look up what your daily caloric intake should be with an app like MyFitnessPal) and burning more calories than you're taking in per day through exercise.

### WANT TO GET HEALTHY?
*Instead of juicing, try eating fruits and vegetables.*
Juice cleanses, in which most nutrients are gained from liquified produce, were among the first to gain popularity among health-conscious Americans. On the surface, juicing can seem like a convenient and time-saving alternative to chopping up a fruit plate. But when squeezed into juice, fruits and vegetables are stripped of the fiber found in their whole form, a nutrient extremely important for your diet and part of the reason why fruit is so healthy. Your juice might have 15 kale leaves in it, but that roughage won't do you as much good in liquid form. "From the standpoint of nutrient density and caloric provision, whole fruit is more nutrient dense," Dr. Kristi Crowe-White, an assistant professor in the University of Alabama's Department of Human Nutrition, told *Outside* magazine in 2013. A recent Harvard study showed whole fruits are also more effective at preventing type 2 diabetes than their liquefied counterparts. Not only is juicing less effective than simply eating a balanced helping of fruits and veggies every day, it's also much less cost-effective. Five days' worth of juices from Juice Press costs $304.98. A high-end juicer can run you more than $100. Juicing is certainly better than skipping fruit altogether, but if you're looking to make a more permanent change, switch out junk food with a healthy snack like almonds or celery and hummus. You could also add fruits and veggies into foods that are already a part of your diet, like yogurt or pasta.

### WANT TO REMOVE TOXINS FROM YOUR BODY?
*Skip cleansing; kick processed foods to the curb.*
There are several degrees of detoxing. It can be as simple as sticking to a pre-planned diet or as complex as the aforementioned Master Cleanse. Regardless of the method, the goal is to rid your body of toxins left behind

by pollution, processed foods and alcohol. But the feeling proponents of cleansing mistake for a detox is actually the feeling of your digestive system going into shock. This can result in debilitating cramps, fatigue and, if you're a frequent cleanser, more serious stomach problems.

Luckily, your body is already very good at cleansing itself of unwanted junk. Chemicals don't just hang around your body—your colon, liver and kidneys help eliminate hard-to-digest food. Militant detox regimens actually get in the way of your body's natural systems for expelling junk. A study in the journal Obesity found that high-glycemic inputs like those found in most cleanses (especially the Master Cleanse, which involves sugary maple syrup) actually make fatty liver buildup more likely than less. But if you do want to make your body's job easier, decrease the amount of processed food—such as frozen meals—you eat and buy organic food instead. The fewer ingredients your choice has on its package, the better. But to ensure the habit sticks, slowly work organic food into your diet, rather than all at once, or your body will still crave the processed food it's used to. Start by making one meal from scratch a week and then build up from there!

## WANT TO FEEL HEALTHIER AND MORE ENERGETIC?
*Instead of juicing, stick to a routine.*
You might think juicing is working because you're skipping through your office and feel like you can work for another four hours, but you're on your way to a major crash. "[It's a] Placebo effect," Dr. Elizabeth Applegate, a professor at University of California at Davis, told *Slate*. "Or ketosis. It's a survival mechanism. You're all amped up and alert because you need something to eat." Living on a liquid diet won't do you any good, but establishing a regimented routine can. Your circadian rhythm—essentially your body's 24-hour internal clock—affects when you feel tired during the day. If you go to bed at midnight one night and 10 p.m. the next, your circadian rhythm doesn't always adjust. This might cause you to lie awake for hours, unable to sleep. Your circadian rhythm is also impacted by when you eat. If you constantly change the times where you fuel up, you'll be hungry at inconvenient times or not hungry when you should be chowing down. You can fix all of this by by waking up, eating and sleeping around the same times each day, which means you can anticipate when you'll need to go on a coffee run, have a nutritious snack or take a 15-minute walk outside to increase your energy.

## NUTRITION

# The Spice of Life?

### Why turmeric is giving hope to millions.

ONE OF THE MOST rewarding parts of seeking out alternative cures and remedies is the realization some of the world's most potentially powerful medicines have been under everyone's noses—or at least our feet—all along. Turmeric, ginger's more colorful and bitter-tasting cousin, has been part of Indian and Southeast Asian cuisine for millennia, but its current place in the spotlight owes more to its potential in the medicine cabinet than its utility on the spice rack.

Studies and anecdotal evidence suggest turmeric can help millions of people struggling with ailments as varied as osteoarthritis to stomach ulcers and even Alzheimer's. "There is increasing evidence on the benefits of turmeric on the brain," Dr. Melissa Young, an integrative medicine specialist at the Cleveland Clinic's Wellness Institute, told *Today*. "Some studies suggest it is helpful in treating depression as well."

Turmeric has been used medicinally in India and Southeast Asia for roughly 4,000 years, and while anyone who's wolfed down a plate of tikka masala can testify to the spice's worth in the kitchen, the plant's medicinal uses have been apparent since people began cultivating it. The ancient users of turmeric would turn to the root to help when suffering from congestion, stomach ailments and more (in Sanskrit, one of the names for turmeric is jayanti, meaning "one who is victorious over diseases"). While modern science has yet to confirm turmeric's effectiveness for solving every medicinal problem its proponents claim it can, recent studies have provided evidence that doses of the plant can help with some of the most common and painful conditions afflicting mankind.

The plant's main ingredient, the curcumin molecule, has been shown to have an anti-inflammatory effect on the body's cells, which could spell relief for the more than 26.9 million Americans suffering from osteoarthritis, the most common form of degenerative joint disease. According to the Arthritis Foundation's website, "a 2010 clinical trial found that a turmeric supplement called Meriva...provided long-term improvement in pain and function in 100 patients with knee OA [osteoarthritis]."

Even if turmeric only helped those suffering from painful joints, that would be more than enough to justify the excitement surrounding the plant in the natural health community. But evidence points to an even bigger role for turmeric—saving lives in addition to relieving pain. A study published in Current Alzheimer Research argues curcumin showed in animals the ability to decrease the spread of amyloids (clusters of proteins) in the brain, which are associated with Alzheimer's.

Animal trials have also hinted that curcumin may help prevent colon, stomach and skin cancers, though much more research is needed before making a definitive conclusion. But that hasn't stopped millions from consuming turmeric—either in powder form with their meals, as a tea or in the form of capsules—and raving about the benefits. If nothing else, it's just one more reason to go ahead and order that chicken tikka masala for dinner tonight.

# Sexual Healing

## When you can't get that feeling, you need natural remedies.

PEOPLE TAKE MEDICINE for a whole host of reasons, but there's little doubt that when you run into a problem in the bedroom, it becomes tempting to turn to Big Pharma to help you put a little pep in your step. According to the Cleveland Clinic, 43 percent of women and 31 percent of men suffer from some form of sexual dysfunction. But not everyone wants a drug-enhanced performance, and some would rather seek out natural remedies to some of mankind's oldest problems. Fortunately, Mother Nature has provided the tools needed to get down to business (or to the business of getting down).

According to a study published in *Association for Psychological Science*, a positive relationship exists between how frequently a couple has sex and how strongly each member of the couple associates their partner with complimentary phrases in a controlled test, underlying the importance of what goes on in the bedroom.

### TRIBULUS TERRESTRIS

This spiny plant found throughout the Mediterranean region may provide the key to helping millions of women find more joy in their love life. Since at least the 18th century, people have been using the plant to help women with lagging libidos, and a recent study suggests there may be something to the centuries-old treatment. Sixty-seven women with hypoactive sexual disorder (basically, a lack of desire for sex) received either a placebo or Tribulus terrestris extract to take. By the end of the study, those receiving the herbal treatment reported an increase in arousal and desire.

### PANAX GINSENG

Though ginseng was most likely discovered thousands of years earlier, the third century saw such a high demand for the root in China it helped bolster the country's international trade. As time has passed, demand for ginseng has only grown, with the plant anchoring a nearly $2.1 billion industry. Evidence suggests ginseng can help men dealing with a certain wilting quality stand at attention. In one study, men given 900 milligrams of ginseng three times a day for eight weeks reported less trouble with their erectile dysfunction.

### PEPPERMINT OIL

Do you gear up to run a marathon but are surprised (and disappointed) to find you're about to run a 50-yard dash instead? You may want to turn to peppermint oil to help you (or your partner) go the distance. When mixed with a carrier oil (such as olive oil, for example), it can be applied directly to the male member to increase sexual stamina. The natural numbing effects of the oil can help make sure you see things through to the end.

NUTRITION

# Eating for Cancer

Why nutrition is playing more of a role in treatment—and prevention—of the disease.

THE VAST MAJORITY of the estimated 1.6 million Americans who were newly diagnosed with some form of cancer last year had their lives forever changed, no doubt forced to reckon with overwhelming feelings of uncertainty, helplessness and fear. It's estimated disease cost more than 600,000 Americans their lives in 2016, and it remains one of the most serious medical threats a person can confront in his or her lifetime. For this reason, oncologists continue to create a barrage of treatments in their fight against the Big C ranging from the dramatic, like blasting the body with radiation, to the mundane, like telling their patients to eat well.

"While perhaps a third of all cancers are related to dietary factors, only a few people in contemporary American medicine realize that a well-structured, nutritional regimen may be useful in the treatment of cancer as well as essential in cancer prevention," writes Dr. Keith Block, co-founder of the Block Center Integrative Cancer Treatment, in the newsletter *Nutrition Digest*. The field is not unanimous in its endorsement, however, and while treatment through diet is causing excitement for some, it's eliciting cries of quackery from others.

The vast majority of medical professionals remain skeptical of claims that proper nutrition alone can drive cancer into

A healthy diet is the first line of defense for cancer prevention. A 2014 study in *The Lancet* revealed a connection between a gain of 34 pounds and a 10 percent increase in the risk of colon cancer.

remission—citing the dearth of evidence backing up such assertions—but mainstream science has by-and-large come to a consensus that what patients eat and drink affects how they react to treatments. "With a healthy diet, you'll go into treatment with reserves to help keep up your strength, prevent body tissue from breaking down, rebuild tissue and maintain your defenses against infection," the American Cancer Society posts on its website. "In fact, some cancer treatments work better in people who are well-nourished and are getting enough calories and protein." In other words, while an apple a day might keep the doctor away, a better rule to keep your oncologist happy is to never skip breakfast and make sure you're eating enough grilled chicken breasts.

The vague nature of the ACS's recommendations on what exactly to eat if one wants to ward off cancer reflects how personal nutrition is, and how any truly effective diet plan needs to be created in conjunction with nutritional experts. But in general, what's healthy for the general population is also what's good for cancer patients, meaning those battling the disease should continue to load up on green, leafy vegetables, lean proteins and healthy fats. One study conducted at the Albert Einstein College of Medicine trying to determine if cancer patients undergoing treatment benefit from a special diet found some evidence that shows restricting carbohydrates (and therefore reducing the amount of insulin the body produces) slowed cancer growth in some patients.

Though the question of prevention through diet is still a contentious one, there's a solid and growing body of evidence that what we eat can help us ward off cancer before it strikes. Again, rather than working on promises of miracle foods that can protect the body against all forms of the disease, a diet aimed at cancer prevention needs to incorporate a variety of foods to help reduce the risk. For example, according to a study in *British Medical Journal*, for every 10 grams of fiber consumed daily (found in whole grains such as oatmeal and brown rice), the risk of contracting colon cancer lowers by 10 percent. A cancer-conscious consumer should also be wary of processed meats, such as hot dogs, ham and bacon, which the International Agency for Research on Cancer classified as a carcinogen (studies found consuming 50 grams of those meats every day increased the risk of colorectal cancer by 18 percent). It's just one more reason to think before you eat.

# Avoiding the Acid

**Why alkaline-based diets have taken the nutrition world by storm.**

WHEN MANKIND'S earliest ancestor climbed down from the treetops thousands of years ago, they did not find a McDonald's hamburger and a Big Gulp of Mountain Dew waiting for them. While that fact may be obvious, it's easy to mistake 21st century access to abundant food and shelter as Homo sapiens' natural state. But the bodies that evolved over millions of years were formed in the crucible of starvation, disease and violence that characterizes the vast majority of human history. Simply put, humanity's talent for invention has far outpaced the inexorable but slow-moving hand of natural selection.

This mismatch has led many to conclude the heaps of processed foods and mountains of protein most residents of the developed world consume on a daily basis may be responsible for a whole host of health problems. Their solution is to plan their meals to return their bodies to a natural balance. One method of achieving such harmony that has gained recent popularity is an alkaline diet. "I think [my diet is] responsible for me not being in pain," host Kelly Ripa exclaimed on her show in 2015 after trying the alkaline diet.

The premise underpinning the alkaline diet is that certain foods cause the body to generate acid, which damages the internal organs. Dieters endeavor to cut down or eliminate

# NUTRITION

Most leafy greens, including kale, lettuce and broccoli, have high pH levels. Brussels sprouts are one of the few greens on the lower end of the pH scale, with a 6.0 level.

consumption of these foods and beverages to make their bodies more alkaline. For anyone who slept through 7th-grade chemistry, anything registering less than 7 on the pH scale (such as coffee) is considered acidic, while anything greater than 7 (such as milk) is considered alkaline. Practically, this means adherents of the alkaline diet need to pile their plates high with fruits, vegetables and plant-based sources of protein such as tofu, while staying away from sugar, the majority of grains, processed foods and (maybe most difficult of all) the twin lures of caffeine and alcohol. In addition to these dietary restrictions, the alkaline-based lifestyle requires testing one's urine multiple times a day to monitor the body's pH levels (with the ideal reading ranging from 7.2 to 7.4).

The benefits, according to the testimonies of those who swear by the alkaline diet, are more than worth the trouble. Reducing the body's acidity can help dieters shed pounds like a sheepdog sheds hair—and some believe it can ward off cancer. Established medical science takes a more skeptical stance about the alkaline diet's extraordinary claims. While certain studies have hinted at a relationship between an alkaline-based diet and the reduction of bone loss, most doctors and nutritionists point to the body's ability to maintain its own pH level.

"The food that you eat does not affect your blood pH," Lauri Wright, Ph.D., a registered dietitian, told *Prevention*. However, nobody disputes the benefits of eating more fresh fruit and vegetables. "The key benefits of this approach seem to stem from guidelines you've already heard a million times: Eat more fruits, veggies and plants; cut back or cut out sugar and processed foods; and slash your sodium intake," dietitian Cynthia Sass wrote in an article posted on *Health.com*. In other words, the alkaline diet may work, but not for the reasons its true believers think.

# The Perilous Path of Sugar

The average American eats about 3 pounds of sugar a week, with adults consuming more than three times the daily recommended intake of 6 teaspoons. Here's what happens every time you take a big gulp of a sweet soda.

**HEAD** Sugar can trigger an addiction-like reaction in the brain for some. A study at Yale University of these addictive eaters showed that just seeing a milk shake catalyzed the same physical response as cocaine. Even in non-addicted brains, sugar suppresses the activity of a hormone called BDNF (brain-derived neurotrophic factor) that is already low in individuals with depression and schizophrenia. In addition, sugar can worsen anxiety symptoms, impair the body's ability to cope with stress and affect sleeping patterns.

**EYES** Every year, between 12,000 and 24,000 people lose their sight to diabetes, which damages the blood vessels that supply the retinas.

**MOUTH** Impacting the body from the start, the sugar in soda is a main contributor to cavities. Sugar also causes the plaque on your teeth to produce acids that attack tooth enamel.

**HEART** Sugar has been found to increase cardiac tissue inflammation, which can damage the heart and result in heart disease.

**LIVER** After ingestion, sugar moves to the liver, where it is broken down. An oversupply in the liver results in its

# NUTRITION

conversion to fat—or, when there's a consistent overload, too much sugar can lead to diabetes.

**PANCREAS** An over-large waistline is the most visible evidence of sugar overindulgence. Sugar is a leading contributor to obesity, which affects more than a third of the U.S. population.

**STOMACH** Diabetes starts like this: If an overload of sugar is ingested, the liver signals the pancreas to pump out copious amounts of insulin—the hormone that helps cells use the broken-down sugar for energy. In people who have insulin resistance, cells can't use insulin effectively, so the pancreas has to keep pumping out more. Eventually, the pancreas can't keep up, and the result is type 2 diabetes. Approximately 21 million Americans were diagnosed with diabetes in 2012, and it is the cause of more deaths than breast cancer and AIDS combined.

**INTESTINE** Neutrophils—the part of the immune system that destroys invading particles like pathogens—are weakened when too much sugar is present. Sugar also interferes with the transport of vitamin C from the intestine, further hobbling the immune system.

**SKIN** Sugar can damage collagen, a protein in the skin that accounts for 30 percent of the body's protein. Once springy-and-resilient collagen is damaged, it becomes dry and brittle, resulting in wrinkles

**LOWER LIMBS** About 60 to 70 percent of people with diabetes have mild to severe forms of diabetes-related nerve damage, which can lead to lower-limb amputations.

# Drink This and That

A breakdown of how coffee and wine, in the right amounts, can be good for you.

## WHY COFFEE?

Coffee has become an essential part of the day for many Americans. In fact, 54 percent of Americans over the age of 18 drink it daily. That's good, because consumption of java just may help lower the risk of some chronic diseases, such as Alzheimer's, type 2 diabetes and cancer. Coffee is even the main source of antioxidants in the Western diet, according to studies—it doesn't have the most, but we are able to absorb the most from it. Loaded with riboflavin, along with a lovely smell to wake up to, your cup of joe offers these numerous health benefits.

- **Research shows** people who drink three to five cups of coffee per day decrease their chance of developing Alzheimer's disease or dementia in their later years by 65 percent.
- **Four or more cups** of coffee a day can help protect the liver against cirrhosis. Some studies have equated it with a 20 percent lower risk.
- **Harvard studies suggest** that women who drink four or more cups of coffee a day have a 20 percent less chance of becoming depressed and a lower risk of developing skin cancer.
- **Coffee increases epinephrine,** or adrenaline, which can improve physical performance by 11 to 12 percent.
- **Japanese studies show** men who drink one to two cups of coffee reduce their

chances of dying from cardiovascular disease by 38 percent.
- **Two large studies** show coffee drinkers have a considerably lower risk of premature death and live longer than those who don't drink it.
- **Coffee can cause** a mild increase in blood pressure, which usually goes away with time and continued usage. Studies show coffee does not increase the risk of heart attack but does decrease the risk of stroke.
- **Several studies** indicate coffee is a good way to burn fat and can increase the metabolism rates by around 11 percent.
- **Harvard researchers** documented the coffee consumption of 40,000 men between 1986 and 1998. They found coffee drinkers had a significantly lowered risk of developing type 2 diabetes, hovering around 50 percent.
- **Coffee induces** a stimulant effect that can increase your energy level, lift your mood and boost overall brain functionality.

## WHY WINE?

Resveratrol, an antioxidant found in the skin of grapes used to make red wine, may make drinking a glass a day a heart health boon. Studies suggest that resveratrol can help reduce heart disease. Other studies suggest that alcohol in general can help produce changes in blood pressure, lower cholesterol, increase high-density lipoprotein (HDL, or good cholesterol) and help protect the arteries when used in moderation. The American Heart Association defines moderate consumption as one to two 4-ounce glasses per day for wine, 12 ounces per day for beer and 1.5 ounces per day for any 80-proof distilled spirits (such as vodka). And the health studies don't skimp on specific benefits. Here's some of the arguments that are pro tippling in moderation.

- **According to** Stony Brook University studies, a daily cup of red wine can cut the risk of colon cancer by 45 percent.
- **Columbia University** studies show the possibility of blood-clot-related strokes decrease by an astounding 50 percent for moderate drinkers.
- **Harvard studies** show moderate drinkers who suffer from high blood pressure decrease the risk of having a heart attack by 30 percent compared to nondrinkers.
- **Studies from Columbia** University saw a significantly faster decline in brain function among those who do not drink than those who do.

NUTRITION

# Growing a Better Brain

Simple garden herbs may help us stay sharp well into old age.

THE HUMAN BRAIN can perform complex computations with an efficiency that still rivals the most powerful supercomputers on the planet. But like all things, this marvelous organ eventually decays, taking with it small memories or our entire identity.

Mainstream medicine spends billions of dollars every year on treatments and research for preserving and protecting the mind. Though established science still has work to do in confirming their efficacy, many herbs and plants may help protect the brain from the ravages of time, and even boost its performance for healthy people.

## CENTELLA ASIATICA

Also known as gotu kola, this herb was first used in India as part of that country's traditional medicine before spreading across the globe. In 2003, a study showed Centella asiatica enhanced cognitive function and relieved oxidant stress (which is associated with Alzheimer's disease) in rats, pointing toward potential benefits in humans.

## GINKGO BILOBA

Ginkgo trees have been on the planet for more than 1,000 years. Recent studies suggest this

- **Studies from** Queen Mary University demonstrate the benefits of procyanidins (condensed tannins—or those things that make you pucker) in red wine, which help protect against heart disease. Wines from southwest France or Sardinia are said to have more procyanidins than others.
- **A Finnish study** conducted on 2,468 men over a 29-year period showed that wine drinkers had a lower rate of mortality by 34 percent over those who exclusively consumed beer or spirits.
- **An Icelandic study** saw a 32 percent decrease in cataract risk among moderate drinkers; wine drinkers fared 43 percent better than beer drinkers.
- **Research on more** than 350,000 subjects at Amsterdam's VU Medical Center indicated that drinking in moderation can decrease the risk of developing type 2 diabetes by 30 percent.

plant can help humans live longer, better lives by treating complications of dementia and Alzheimer's. Not only does ginkgo help open blood vessels and thin the blood, which may help alleviate vascular dementia caused by improper blood flow to the brain, but there's also evidence it may protect the nerves that come under attack during Alzheimer's. An analysis of several studies published on the National Center for Biotechnology Information's website concluded the plant was more effective than a placebo in treating the disease, though the Alzheimer's Association has yet to find a statistical difference between ginkgo biloba and placebo tests. It's still nevertheless a promising starting point for further exploration.

## LESSER PERIWINKLE

This shrub is not only pleasing to the eye but may also help the brain. The plant contains vincamine, an alkaloid that according to the University of Michigan has been "shown to be beneficial" for people suffering from Alzheimer's in a double-blind trial. Another double-blind study has shown the plant can benefit those suffering from mild vascular dementia, as stated in a review published on the National Institute of Health's website.

## ASHWAGANDHA

This root originating in India is used to treat many ailments. Studies indicate ashwagandha can help boost cognitive function. One study published in *Natural Medicine Journal* showed subjects taking the substance for 14 days performed better on a psychomotor test.

NUTRITION

# How to Keep Alzheimer's at Bay

A guide to safeguarding your brain's future health.

SINCE IT WAS FIRST described by German psychiatrist Alois Alzheimer in 1906, the brain-degenerating disease that bears his name has baffled scientists and wrecked the lives of countless sufferers and those close to them. Experts at the Marcus Neuroscience Institute at Boca Raton Regional Hospital, including Dr. James A. Galvin, are developing an understanding of the disease. Thankfully for the world—an estimated 1 in 85 adults will develop the disease by 2050—that includes strategies for managing your risk for Alzheimer's. Try these tips from Dr. Galvin to optimize your brain's health for years to come.

## SIX STEPS TO HELPING STAVE OFF ALZHEIMER'S

### 1. FOCUS ON RISK REDUCTION

"There is a growing interest in risk-reduction strategies to try to lower the incidence rate of new Alzheimer's disease cases," Galvin says. "Of course, the greatest risk factor is age, followed by genetics and family history, none of which are modifiable. After these, the strongest risk factors for Alzheimer's are things you can actually be quite proactive about—namely lifestyle choices like diet, exercise and social and cognitive stimulation."

### 2. KEEP TABS ON OTHER DISEASES

Other major risk factors for Alzheimer's disease are actually the illnesses that happen simultaneously, according to Galvin. Chronic conditions like diabetes, hypertension, high cholesterol, obesity and sleep disorders can all add to the risk of developing Alzheimer's if left untreated.

### 3. KNOW THERE'S NO SILVER BULLET FOR THE DISEASE

"It is difficult to say what will prevent Alzheimer's disease because there are people who have followed similar 'recipes' their whole lives—marathon-running or eating vegan, for example—who develop Alzheimer's," Galvin says, "and people who have never done any of these things—who eat Twinkies, chain-smoke and become couch potatoes—who never develop AD. Rather than looking for a combination to prevent disease, we should do what we can to reduce risk."

### 4. TAKE HEART
Heart-healthy choices also tend to be brain-healthy choices, Galvin says. A steady supply of oxygenated blood helps maximize brain health. "Despite all the advances in medications and diagnostics [to specifically combat Alzheimer's], sometimes the best things we can tell a patient are to stay mentally active, socially engaged and physically fit and eat a healthy diet," Galvin says.

### 5. KNOW THE WARNING SIGNS
There are several indicators of AD that have been identified and can help the disease's victims know when to seek treatment. According to the Alzheimer's Association, some of the top warning signs are:
- Memory loss that disrupts the flow of daily life
- Misplacing things and losing the ability to retrace steps
- Difficulty completing familiar tasks at home, at work or at leisure
- Confusion with time or place
- Trouble understanding visual images and spatial relationships

### 6. TREAT IT EARLY
Don't delay getting a diagnosis out of fear. Galvin adds that there are a number of benefits to early detection of Alzheimer's, including the ability to start medications at the earliest possible stage, which may help reduce the memory loss and confusion symptoms of the disease. There is also the possibility of participating in clinical trials to test new therapies and medications. In the past few years, several drugs have shown positive signs of slowing Alzheimer's.

# The Tao of Tea

**An ancient elixir could be the all-purpose natural supplement you've been seeking.**

APART FROM GOOD old hydrogen dioxide, tea in all its forms constitutes the most widely consumed beverage on Earth. People have been drinking tea for thousands of years, and it has always been both an enjoyable beverage and an elixir renowned for its healing properties. In fact, tea has long been considered integral to a well-balanced, naturally based lifestyle, as shown in the Japanese proverb, "If man has no tea in him, he is incapable of understanding truth and beauty." There are a wide variety of teas, each with its own unique health benefits as well as flavor profiles. The beverage contains antioxidants, properties that prevent cancer, immune-system building components and heart-healthy nutrients, as well as many other positive and healthy attributes.

### BLACK
With about 40 milligrams of caffeine per cup, black tea is among the most caffeinated varieties. Made with fermented leaves, it contains cholesterol-lowering antioxidants and may lower one's risk of stroke.

### GREEN
Made with steamed tea leaves, green tea can help reduce the likelihood of stroke

and different neurological diseases, as well as burn fat and lower cholesterol. The healthy antioxidants can even help prevent a variety of cancers and tumor growths. This incredible drink also helps to prevent tooth decay and cardiovascular disease.

### WHITE
Uncured and unfermented, white tea goes through very little processing. It can help fight cancer and cardiovascular disease, and it is great for dental health. It is also a good source of antioxidants.

### OOLONG
Some antioxidants in oolong tea have been shown to lower cholesterol levels. The tea helps to activate the enzymes that break down triglycerides, a fat found in the bloodstream. Oolong also contains properties that help detoxify the body and can prevent tooth decay.

### PU-ERH
A type of black tea, pu-erh tea is made from fermented and aged leaves, which are pressed into cakes. It can help to lower cholesterol and increase alertness.

### CHAMOMILE
This stress-reducing herbal tea can help those who suffer from insomnia. Chamomile also prevents complications that stem from diabetes.

### ECHINACEA
The antioxidants in echinacea, an herbal tea, can boost immunity, which can help you combat the common cold and may prevent you from coming down with one in the first place.

### ROOIBOS
A red tea, rooibos is a fermented herb from South Africa. It is packed with vitamins, minerals and antioxidants, and it can aid in stress reduction and help those who suffer from insomnia get a restful sleep.

### LEMONGRASS
Citral, which is contained in lemongrass, helps with food digestion, making this tea a good choice for your gastrointestinal health.

### GINGER
Ginger tea acts as an anti-inflammatory, which is ideal for arthritis. It also helps with nausea relief as well as digestion and can help to alleviate congestion—something to keep in mind during cold season.

### PEPPERMINT
Peppermint is a wonder tea for anyone feeling ill. It immediately helps with mild coughs or asthma, congestion and mild

aches, and it can sooth those suffering from vomiting, nausea and motion sickness while strengthening overall immunity. The menthol in peppermint tea also helps combat stress and anxiety, as it is a muscle relaxant.

**ROSE HIP**
Made from the fruit of the rose plant, rose hip tea is chock-full of vitamin C and helps boost the immune system.

**LAVENDER**
A medicinal herb, lavender has a wide variety of health benefits. It's especially helpful in terms of respiratory issues and can be used to help soothe coughs, asthma and bronchitis. Its healing properties help heal sores, cuts, wounds and ulcers.

**MILK THISTLE**
Milk thistle tea is great for liver health, both cleaning one's liver and improving its function. It can also help lower cholesterol and blood sugar levels, which makes the tea a useful beverage for those with cardiovascular issues or type 2 diabetes.

**DANDELION**
When brewed as tea, dandelions help to lower fluid retention and therefore are great for arthritis patients, as they reduce the pain associated with arthritic swelling. The tea contains a ton of vitamins and minerals, and helps improve liver function and the health of one's digestive system.

**CINNAMON**
This tea helps to control blood sugar and cholesterol levels, and is great for weight loss. It also helps increase the body's strength for fighting some viruses.

# Notes

# Fitness

Keep yourself moving and stay hydrated to see how your body in motion doesn't just stay in motion—it strengthens your heart, improves your memory and more.

FITNESS

# The No-Excuses Exercise Guide

There's always a reason why you can't work out, but here's a plan (and personalized playlists) that'll bust every one of them.

THE EXCUSE
## "I'M WAAAAAY TOO BUSY."

You're closing deals from the time the rooster crows to the wee hours and helping kids with homework in between, so there's simply not enough time in a day.

**THE WORKOUT**
If efficiency is your middle name, stick to full-body exercises, such as swimming laps, to get the maximum workout in the least amount of time. Stuck on an assignment? Studies suggest people who squeeze in exercise in the middle of their day are more productive (20 minutes on a treadmill at lunch fits the bill). Can't leave home without little ones in tow? Do crunches in the living room.

**PRO TIPS**
To maintain a healthy lifestyle, you should take at least 10,000 steps a day in addition to your workout. If you commute, hop off the train a few stops early or park your car at the far end of the lot. If you get a long phone call, take it on the go. Walk around the office, or march in place by your desk. Chasing the kids around is a good workout, too. But you knew that already.

THE PLAYLIST
## POWER LUNCH
Sweat out the day's stress by crushing your air guitar to these classics.

"Eye of the Tiger" Survivor
"You Shook Me All Night Long" AC/DC
"Are You Gonna Go My Way" Lenny Kravitz
"Walk This Way" Run DMC ft. Aerosmith
"Start Me Up" The Rolling Stones
"It's My Life" Bon Jovi
"We're Not Gonna Take It" Twisted Sister
"Click Click Boom" Saliva
"My Way" Limp Bizkit

THE EXCUSE
# "I'M TOO TIRED TO EXERCISE."

After a long day at the office, you usually don't feel like you've got the energy to work out. You can barely lift a finger, much less a dumbbell.

**THE WORKOUT**
If you're looking for an instant energy boost, try yoga, Pilates or tai chi. These workouts use deliberate movements and strength training to increase your energy. If you're ready for something a little more intense, create a rockin' playlist to psych yourself up. (Or use the one we made for you!) Listening to music during high-intensity exercise can reduce tension and change your mood. You might even want to try an activity that integrates music and movement, like Zumba.

## THE PLAYLIST
## RISE & GRIND
A cup of coffee for your ears for those who need musical motivation to get moving.

- **"'Till I Collapse"** Eminem
- **"Can't Hold Us"** Macklemore & Ryan Lewis
- **"Radioactive"** Imagine Dragons
- **"Victory"** Puff Daddy ft. Busta Rhymes & Notorious B.I.G.
- **"Stronger"** Kanye West
- **"Holy Grail"** Jay-Z ft. Justin Timberlake
- **"Hustler's Ambition"** 50 Cent
- **"Big Things Poppin'"** T.I.
- **"Remember the Name"** Fort Minor

**PRO TIPS**
Though high-intensity exercise is best for improving long-term energy levels, it can make you temporarily exhausted. But moderate exercise can actually increase your energy. A 15-minute walk has more instant energy benefits than a 45-minute run because it wakes up your system without tiring it out. Even a walk around the room will make you feel refreshed and recharged.

# FITNESS

### THE EXCUSE
## "I'D RATHER NOT WASTE MONEY ON A FANCY GYM MEMBERSHIP OR EXPENSIVE AT-HOME EQUIPMENT."

Unless there's a deal for a pass to the fitness center, you're not going. You're thrifty, resourceful and see no reason to pay for something you can get for free.

### THE WORKOUT
You can get a complete burn without leaving the house. Jog up and down the stairs to get a cardio workout that also tones your lower body. Alternate sets of wall sits and standing wall push-ups to tone your whole body. Bicycles, lunges and planks are also great exercises that engage different muscle groups.

### PRO TIPS
Get tidy and toned—and get your chores done simultaneously. Vacuuming, changing bedsheets and mopping engage a variety of muscles and increase your heart rate. When you run errands, consider actually running to do them. And if you do want to splurge a little, popular at-home workout plans (such as P90X) are significantly cheaper than a gym membership.

---

### THE PLAYLIST
## IRON MAN
Rocky Balboa didn't defeat Apollo Creed for the heavy-weight title by sitting on the couch. You shouldn't either.

- **"Gonna Fly Now"** Bill Conti
- **"Stayin' Alive"** Bee Gees
- **"KernKraft 400"** Zombie Nation
- **"Call Me"** Blondie
- **"Iron Man"** Black Sabbath
- **"Sandstorm"** Darude
- **"Back in Black"** AC/DC
- **"Mama Said Knock You Out"** LL Cool J
- **"Gonna Make You Sweat (Everybody Dance Now)"** C+C Music Factory

## THE EXCUSE
## "I'LL ADMIT IT: I'M TOO LAZY."

Gym who? The lure of streaming whole seasons of nearly every show that's ever existed is too tempting an alternative. If only there were a way you could get fit and find out what happens to Eleven.

### THE WORKOUT
Multitask by turning TV time into exercise time. Make a pact to only watch your favorite shows while you're on a treadmill or stationary bike. No fancy equipment? During commercials, get off the couch and do a quick set of jumping jacks or mountain climbers. Binge-streaming on Netflix? Do three sets of 15 push-ups, crunches or dips before the start of any new episode.

### PRO TIPS
Breaking routines can be tough. Remind yourself of your fitness goals by moving some exercise equipment near your couch. It'll be harder to binge on your favorite shows with a pair of dumbbells quietly taunting you.

## THE PLAYLIST
## SPRING CLEANING
If you're planning on working out while sprucing up, this is the soundtrack.

**"I Love It"** Icona Pop ft. Charli XCX
**"Barbra Streisand"** Duck Sauce
**"Jump Around"** House of Pain
**"The Way You Move"** Outkast
**"Feel So Good"** Mase
**"Move Your Feet"** Junior Senior
**"Reptilia"** The Strokes
**"Pursuit of Happiness (Steve Aoki Remix)"** Kid Cudi ft. MGMT & Ratatat

THE EXCUSE
## "I HATE WORKING OUT ALONE."

You've tried to stick to a plan before but find that without someone to keep you accountable (and to chat with), you bail. And you're not interested in paying a personal trainer.

**THE WORKOUT**
You can arrange a quick and easy group exercise by setting up a circuit-training loop. Invite friends over and arrange four to six stations, each assigned a different exercise. Do a five-minute cardio boost together, such as jumping jacks or jogging in place. Then each of you starts at a different station and performs a workout such as mountain climbers, squats or bicep curls. Move stations every two minutes.

**PRO TIPS**
Working out with a group means you're more likely to push yourself and stick to a routine. Check out the group exercise classes at your local gym and pick something you've never tried before. Instead of meeting a friend for coffee or a beer, arrange to hang out on a tennis court or at a ball field.

THE PLAYLIST
## GAME DAY
A dynamic playlist for the dynamic duo of you and your workout buddy. Skip the earbuds and crank up the stereo.

**"Joker and the Thief"** Wolfmother
**"Thunderstruck"** AC/DC
**"We Will Rock You"** Queen
**"Crazy Train"** Ozzy Osbourne
**"Song 2"** Blur
**"Banquet"** Bloc Party
**"Seven Nation Army"** The White Stripes
**"Welcome to the Jungle"** Guns N' Roses
**"Party Rock Anthem"** LMFAO

FITNESS

THE EXCUSE
## "I GOTTA BE HONEST: WORKING OUT IS BORING."

The view from a treadmill never changes. The track is the same circle over and over. Crunches are just lying down and sitting up.

**THE WORKOUT**
Cross-training is a great way to keep your body guessing and your mind engaged. Changing the type of exercise you do also increases your endurance, strength and flexibility. Switch up your workout during the week: cardio one day, weights the next. You can also change things up during the workout. If you want to do 30 minutes of cardio, split your time evenly between the treadmill, bike and rowing machine.

**PRO TIPS**
Find an activity that doesn't feel like exercise. Hiking is a great cardio workout that has better views than the inside of a gym. If you want to stay closer to home, test out your green thumb. Gardening uses movements that require endurance, flexibility and strength.

---

THE PLAYLIST
## NEVER A DULL MOMENT

Spice up your workout routine with these frenetic, kinetic dance numbers.

- **"NRG"** Duck Sauce
- **"Danza Kuduro"** Don Omar ft. Lucenzo
- **"Calabria"** Enur ft. Natasja
- **"Take Over Control"** Afrojack ft. Eva Simons
- **"Y.a.l.a."** M.I.A.
- **"Watch Out for This (Bumaye)"** Major Lazer
- **"Walking on Air"** Katy Perry
- **"212"** Azealia Banks
- **"Run the World (Girls)"** Beyoncé
- **"We Found Love"** Rihanna ft. Calvin Harris

FITNESS

# All About Acupuncture

With its potential head-to-toe benefits, the popular Eastern medicine practice of pricking the skin with needles may keep your health on-point.

## BRAIN

Acupuncture may provide relief from a variety of mental health issues, ranging from mild cases of stress to bouts of depression. In a study conducted at the University of Arizona, 34 women with depression underwent targeted acupuncture, which treats a specific area of the body, generalized acupuncture, which provides varying benefits throughout the body, or no treatment at all. Reduced symptoms were seen in 43 percent of the women who received acupuncture for depression and in 22 percent of those who received general acupuncture. Eight weeks after the start of the study, more than half of the women who received targeted acupuncture were no longer experiencing depression. Some credit the Eastern practice's success to its perceived ability to release endorphins, which act as natural painkillers within the body—as well as acupuncture's potential to reduce the stress hormone cortisol.

## LUNGS

A study published in the August 2012 edition of the *Natural Medicine Journal* and touted by the Lung Institute examined the effects of acupuncture on 68 sufferers of Chronic Obstructive Pulmonary Disease (COPD), a form of lung disease restricting airflow. Over the course of 12 weeks, half of COPD patients received legitimate acupuncture treatments while the other half were administered placebo procedures involving needles that did not puncture the skin. The study revealed far less breathlessness in the group given actual treatments, which one of the researchers, Masao Suzuki of Kyoto University in Japan, explained by stating, "Acupuncture causes relaxation of these muscles and, consequently, the function of the muscles recovers to support better respiration."

## DIGESTIVE SYSTEM

Acupuncture has long been used to treat stomach problems. In a study examining

59 studies conducted between 1986 and 2015, the Cochrane Collaboration found the effectiveness of wrist PC6 acupuncture point stimulation for postoperative cases of nausea and vomiting to be comparable overall to that of anti-nausea drugs.

**SPINE**
One of the most common problems causing people to seek out an acupuncturist is chronic back pain. For thousands of years, chronic back pain has been treated with traditional acupuncture, using thin needles that are inserted into various points in the back. But in a 2008 case series published in the *Evidence-Based Complementary and Alternative Medicine* journal, electroacupuncture—a modified form of the treatment that involves a tiny, pulsating electrical current—was conducted on patients with lumbar spinal stenosis in lieu of standard acupuncture. The patients each experienced varying reductions in lower back pain, and the distance they were able to walk increased.

**SKELETAL SYSTEM**
Arthritis, a disease that causes painful inflammation and stiffness of the joints, ranks near the top of the list of complaints driving people to acupuncture centers. According to a 2008 *Arthritis & Rheumatology* review of eight acupuncture studies involving 536 patients with rheumatoid arthritis, "five studies revealed a reduction in erythrocyte sedimentation rate (ESR), three reported a reduction in C-reactive protein (CRP) and one noted a large decrease in both." As both ESR and CRP are markers of inflammation in the body, researchers have highlighted the potential of acupuncture as a valuable form of rheumatoid arthritis treatment.

# How to Stay Hydrated

### An easy-to-follow guide that ensures your body is a well-watered machine.

ONE OF THE single most important—and easiest—things you can do for your body is drink enough water. Everything in your body needs water to keep functioning, from whole organs like the heart and lungs down to the tiniest cells. Water not only flushes out waste, but it also lubricates joints and keeps your eyes, nose and mouth moist enough to see, smell and taste. It's so vital for your body to keep an adequate supply on hand that when you're properly hydrated, water makes up about 60 percent of your body weight.

Because of all those essential uses for water, though, the body has a tendency to run through its storehouse of H2O pretty quickly. Even breathing uses some up. In fact, a human normally loses a total of about 10 cups of fluid a day in just exhaled air, perspiration and bodily secretions. All that loss—without near-constant resupply—can lead to dehydration. A few simple moves can keep you optimally hydrated, though, and help you never go thirsty again.

# EIGHT STEPS TO KEEPING OPTIMALLY HYDRATED

### 1. DO THE MATH
Drink half your body weight in ounces of water a day.

### 2. DRINK EARLY
Don't wait for thirst to hit. By the time you feel the urge to hoist a glass, you're already on your way to dehydration. Thirst only hits after two or more cups of total body water have been lost, according to Pennsylvania's Health and Welfare Wellness Committee.

### 3. SIP SLOW AND STEADY
Don't gulp all the day's water at once; the overload will just have you rushing to the john. Keep a glass or bottle of water handy throughout the entire day.

### 4. ADJUST AS NECESSARY
If you are working out, tack on another 16 to 20 ounces per hour of exertion. According to CrossFit Endurance, 1 percent of dehydration can lower performance 10 to 12 percent.

### 5. BEAT THE HEAT
If the temperature is rising, add another 8 ounces per hour outside. Add 20 or more ounces per hour if you are exercising in the heat.

### 6. SUB IN SOURCES
Having trouble drinking enough water? All beverages and broths are water-based, and fruits and vegetables can also be a good source of $H_2O$, especially watermelon, tomatoes and lettuce, which are more than 90 percent water by weight.

### 7. SPICE UP YOUR ROUTINE
Add some kick to the hydration process to keep it interesting. A slice of lemon, lime or cucumber can add a calorie-free flavor boost to a glass of $H_2O$.

### 8. MAKE A DATE TO DRINK
Older brains may not sense dehydration and lose the ability to send out the signals for thirst. Set times to drink and stick to them.

# Ancient Exercise

Originating in Northern China hundreds of years ago, tai chi is more than a martial art—it's medicine.

**T**AI CHI CHUAN, an ancient Chinese martial art whose name means "Supreme Ultimate Fist," might not seem like the best tool for healing based on these immediate facts. But the activity, known commonly by the shortened name tai chi, has reams of scientific evidence backing its methods of attaining holistic health. Tai chi is recognizable to most westerners as a physical therapy activity most often performed by the infirm and elderly for whom higher-impact exercise is painful or impossible. The activity's benefits in this area are proven as well, but thinking of tai chi simply as kung fu's equivalent of large print novels or the three-wheeled motorcycle causes most of us to miss the full spectrum of benefits offered by tai chi chuan, which according to Harvard University, range from muscle strength and flexibility to respiratory health.

According to the textbook *Sports Around the World: History, Culture, and Practice* by John Nauright and Charles Parrish, tai chi has historical records of its practice dating back to the mid-16th century, when the so-called Chen style originated in the Northern Chinese village of the same name. Since then, all derivative styles have been categorized as "soft" or, more accurately, internal martial arts.

Simply put, "hard" martial arts such as Shaolin style kung fu deploy opposing force as their main weapon. "Soft" martial arts such as aikido, judo and tai chi chuan rely on yielding force—they use an attacker's power against him or her and rely more on focus, balance and mindfulness. Despite tai chi's martial origins, competitive sparring is just one element of the activity, and those with no interest in trading blows can still reap plenty of benefits. Practical modern tai chi focuses on breathing technique and the deliberate repetition of sequences

FITNESS

of movements that result in what some have termed "physical meditation."

Tai chi is a gentle exercise that won't leave a practitioner out of breath even after a full class of movement, but it also does a great deal to strengthen the lungs, limbs and general health of those who commit to its practice. The Mayo Clinic calls tai chi "safe for all ages and fitness levels" and goes on to specify that "you may also find tai chi appealing because it's inexpensive and requires no special equipment."

"Although you aren't working with weights or resistance bands, the unsupported arm exercise involved in tai chi strengthens your upper body," Dr. Gloria Yeh, an assistant professor at Harvard Medical School, told the university's Women's Health Watch. "Tai chi strengthens both the lower and upper extremities and also the core muscles of the back and abdomen." Dr. Yeh also pointed out that the balance skills honed through tai chi can be extremely useful for overall health, whether it's the mental balance proven to reduce stress, or the physical balance shown to decrease risk of falls in the elderly.

When the National Institute of Health published a conclusive study on the health effects of tai chi in 2010, they put it best: "Research has demonstrated consistent, significant results for a number of health benefits." Tai chi and its breathing-centered offshoot qigong, which focuses only on breath control without physical movements and can be practiced at most tai chi centers, offer conditioning on the level of resistance training, but require almost none of the intense exertions that make many martial arts too daunting a task for many. That's a win that should quicken the breath of anyone looking to safely and naturally strengthen their overall health.

# Perks of Posing

The bodily benefits of yoga begin the day you first roll out the mat—and they can last a lifetime.

INNER PEACE and personal pride are among the spiritual fruits that practicing yoga can bear, but many who pose are just as drawn to the physical rewards. Beyond the ability to bend like the St. Louis Gateway Arch, yoga can offer an abundance of other physical advantages. From building a stronger skeleton to bringing blood pressure to lower levels, a venture into the practice can improve health in both the short and long term.

**BRAIN**
With its emphasis on focus, the ancient practice of Hatha yoga—which is devoted to postures rather than sequences—has shown to be effective in increasing cognitive functions. After completing just one 20-minute Hatha yoga session, participants in a 2013 University of Illinois study fared better on tests involving working memory and inhibitory control than those who partook in aerobic exercise for the same amount of time.

**BONES**
Yoga may not only prevent loss of bone mass, but it can also potentially increase bone growth. A study conducted in 2009 by physician and integrative medicine advocate Dr. Loren Fishman revealed that the range of motion

A simple yoga position, such as tree pose, can help aid balance, strengthen your entire body and restore confidence and energy.

developed by practicing yoga can prevent osteoporosis and osteoarthritis later in life.

### LUNGS
According to a study from Ball State University, a 15-week period of Hatha yoga can improve an individual's vital lung capacity. This means they see an increase in the amount of air exhaled from deep breaths—an essential aspect of yoga.

### BLOOD CELLS
In a recent Harvard University study, researchers examined blood samples from one group that practiced mindful meditation and one group that did not. After an eight-week period, 2,209 genes within those in the meditation group showed changes, which largely involved their cells' ability to use oxygen and nutrients and create energy. The results revealed that the meditation aspect of yoga can improve cellular metabolism, which can yield major benefits such as blocking degenerative genetic disorders and lengthening the life of DNA cells.

### MUSCLES
Increased muscle strength is one of the most physically evident benefits of yoga. Beyond the visible results, though, the muscle development yields greater internal advantages such as increased joint support, which can prevent arthritis.

### HEART
The practice of yoga activates a relaxed state, which can result in lower blood pressure and increased blood flow from the heart to the rest of the body. As a long term result, a practicing yogi or yogini may have a lower risk of heart disease, according to a 2014 study in the *European Journal of Preventive Cardiology*.

FITNESS

# Back in Action

An achy lumbar and spine area doesn't have to stop you from practicing yoga. Try these modifications for safe posing.

**A** BAD BACK is one of the most common excuses people present for why they won't try yoga. To many, it seems unfathomable to get into any pose involving an arch, a twist, a bend. But with some slight adjustments, you can safely perform a variety of poses, pain free. You'll likely also start to feel the pain begin to fade entirely.

**STANDING FORWARD BEND**
Unmodified standing forward bends can put a lot of strain on your lower back—especially if you have tight hamstrings. To avoid this, rest your palms on support blocks as you bend over. You can also bend your knees slightly to stretch your hamstrings.

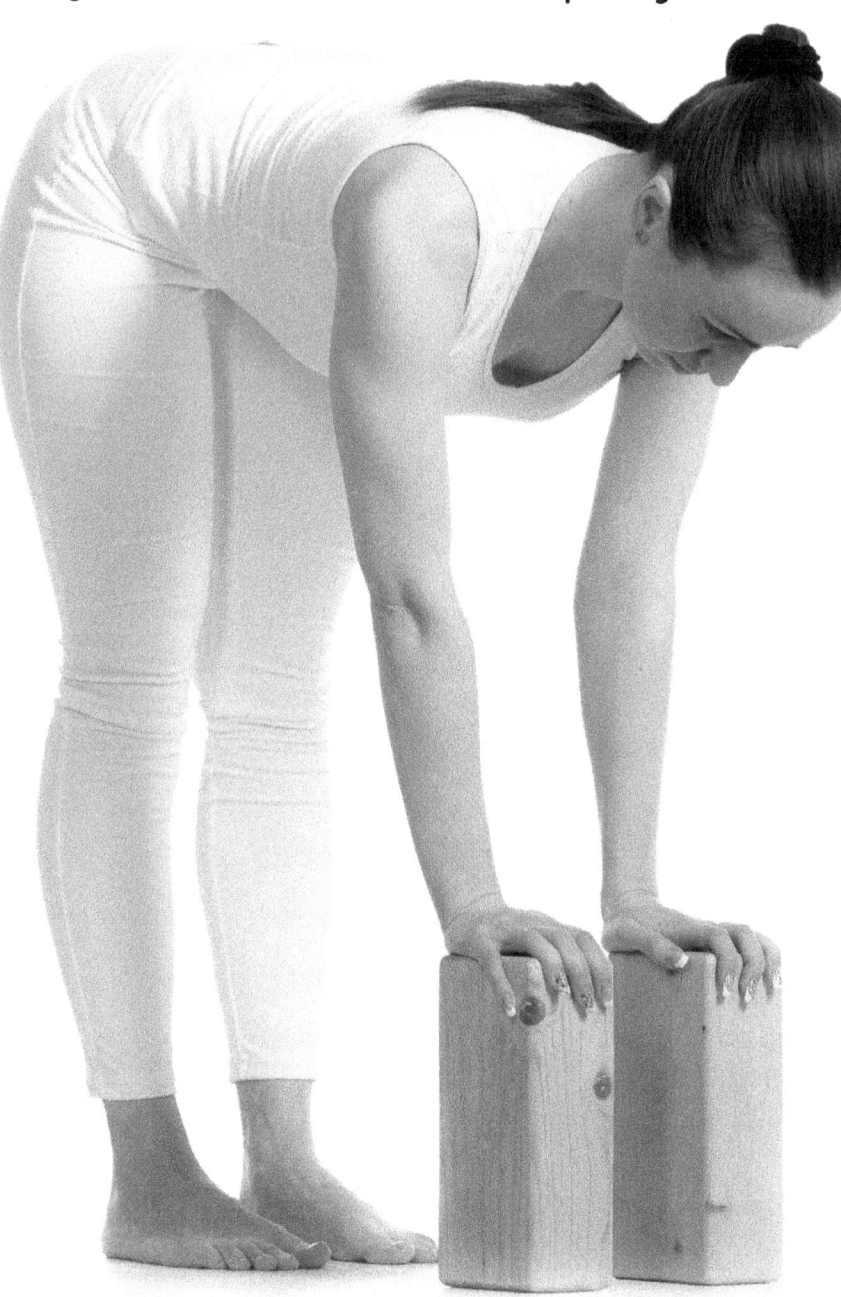

### SPHINX POSE

If you're concerned about risking further back injury by going into cobra pose, try this modification. Rather than rising all the way up on your stomach, rest your hands on the ground with your elbows underneath your shoulders and push yourself up. This pose will stretch your chest nicely and extend your back without tension.

### HEAD-TO-KNEE POSE

This pose can loosen up your hamstrings and, ultimately, your lower back. In a supine position, bend your leg and place your foot on the ground, then wrap your hand around the opposite foot and raise it in the air. If you can't reach your foot, you can use a strap instead.

### CORPSE POSE

Although corpse pose is supposed to be relaxing and help the body unwind after a yoga class, it can be uncomfortable for those with a tight lower back. To avoid this, place a blanket or blocks underneath the knees as you lie flat on the mat, arms relaxed at your side. This will relieve both hip and back stress.

### SUPPORTED CHILD POSE

Sometimes a full child's pose can overextend your lower back, but some support from a blanket will help you get into position safely. Spread your knees and place the blanket between them. Push your hips back to your feet and touch your toes together. Next, fold forward to rest your upper body on the blanket with your head turned to one side. After a few breaths, be sure to turn your head to the other side to get an equal stretch.

FITNESS

# Relaxing Routine
### Some sequences focus on fitness, but this one will simply soothe your stress.

**EASY POSE**
Seated with legs crossed, roll your shoulders back to open your chest and lengthen your spine. Rest your tongue against the roof of your mouth and relax all facial muscles. Take deep breaths through the nose and into the belly and try to devote your entire focus to your breathing. Aim for anywhere from 10 to 30 sustained breaths.

**BOUND ANGLE**
Unite the soles of your feet in bound angle pose and lace your fingers around your toes. Press your elbows into your hips, shoulders back and chest out. Close your eyes and take three to six sustained breaths.

**REVOLVED HEAD TO KNEE**
With your left leg extended out 45 degrees, pull your right foot in toward your hips. Put your left palm on the left leg, then inhale and extend your right arm up to the sky. As you exhale, extend your left-hand fingers to your toes and your right-hand fingers to the left wall, reaching over the ear as you bend. Hold for two to four breaths then slowly inhale, bringing your torso back into upright position. Repeat on opposite side.

### SEATED TWIST
Cross your left foot over your extended right leg with the right elbow placed on the raised left knee. While exhaling, reach your left hand behind you and place your palm and fingers flat on the floor. As you reach, twist your spine and look over your left shoulder. Repeat on opposite side.

### WIND RELIEVING POSE
Wrap your arms around your knees and roll onto your back while bringing the knees to your chest. As you pull the knees in closer, press the back of your neck, shoulders and tailbone into the floor to stretch your lower back. Hold two to five breaths.

### SUPINE BOUND ANGLE
In a supine position, unite the bottoms of your feet. Inhaling, bring your arms up over your head, palms together. You can relax to complete the posture as gravity

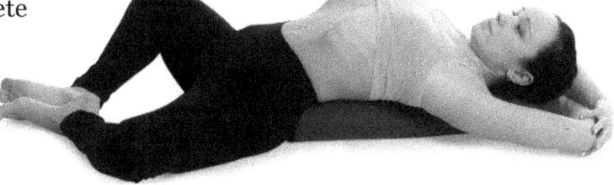

### SHAVASANA/CORPSE POSE
While exhaling, straighten your legs and release your arms into a relaxed position alongside the torso, assuming corpse pose. With your palms turned upward, keep your arms about 7 inches from your body. Close your eyes and relax your entire body from the crown of your head to the tips of your toes. Take deep breaths through the nose and hold for about 10 to 15 minutes.

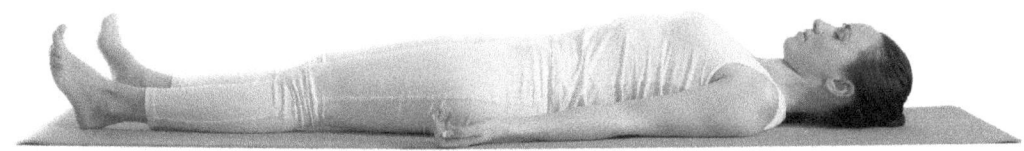

### EASY POSE
Bending your knees, roll over onto one side to push up into the pose, ending as you started the sequence. Relax all facial muscles and focus your mind on breathing, holding 10 to 30 breaths.

FITNESS

# Saluting the Sun

Not a fan of Mondays? Try this sequence in sets of two or three to greet the morning with positive energy.

I F YOU'RE HOPING to start the day with your best foot forward, Sun Salutations are often the way to go. As the name suggests, these poses are traditionally used to welcome the new day—a feat that's often not as easy as it sounds. But if you can get in the habit of rolling out of bed and rolling out your yoga mat to perform these poses, you might find a new appreciation for the morning.

**UPWARD SALUTE**
Standing with your feet rooted with even weight distribution, set a slow, steady breathing rhythm. While inhaling, stretch your arms out to the side and slowly bring them up over your head. Keep your hands open as you reach toward the sky. Hold for one breath.

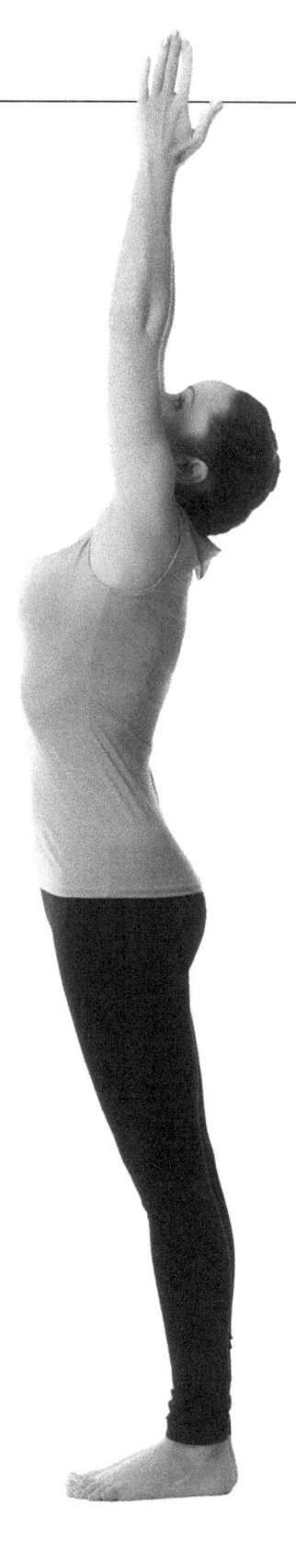

**STANDING FORWARD BEND**
Exhale and bend forward from the hips. Focus on lengthening the front torso as you enter position. If you aren't able to comfortably touch your toes or the floor, you can simply touch your hands to your shins.

**PLANK POSE**
Place your palms flat on the floor with your hands shoulder-width apart and step your feet back one at a time until your body is parallel to the floor, feet hip-width apart. Inhale one full breath and slightly turn your outer arms inward as your index fingers become a firmer root for the pose. Relax your facial muscles as you look down at the mat and exhale.

**UPWARD FACING DOG**
Inhale as you push your chest forward and place the tops of your feet on the floor. With your palms pressed into the floor for support, lift your torso and thighs slightly off the ground as you continue inhaling. After a few seconds, exhale, bringing your lower body back to plank pose.

**DOWNWARD FACING DOG**
Roll over your toes to bring the bottoms of your feet flat on the floor. Keeping your hands slightly out past your shoulders, exhale and bring your knees up off the floor. Slowly straighten your knees until your tailbone is pointed directly up at the sky and hold for five breaths.

**MOUNTAIN POSE**
On breath five, bend your knees and inhale, then step forward between your hands. As you lift your hands from the floor, exhale and rise with your arms at your sides. Continue standing in position for three to four full breaths. Return to Upward Salute to repeat the sequence.

THE ULTIMATE HOLISTIC HANDBOOK FOR BEGINNERS

FITNESS

**6:30 a.m.**
**Have Sex**
Because men are physically primed for intercourse during their last cycle of REM sleep, you might want to give your partner an early wake-up call for an a.m. dose of connectedness and well-being. Sex also releases the hormone oxytocin, which makes you feel more upbeat.

**7:30 a.m.**
**Go for a Run**
Your body's temperature is lower from the previous night's slumber, so exercising close to waking minimizes the risk of heat stroke when engaging in low-intensity, extended exercise such as long-distance running.

**8:30 a.m.**
**Take Care of Business**
While 1,000 different factors, like hydration or a shot of caffeine, influence when it's time to visit the toilet, the rhythms of your intestines make bowel movements most common between 8:00 a.m. and 9:00 a.m.

**Noon**
**Eat Lunch**
A meal loaded with fiber and low in fat will help mitigate the sleepiness from your midafternoon slump and help you resist that container of Double Stuf Oreos someone brought to the office snack room.

**6 a.m.** — **12 p.m.**

**7:00 a.m.**
**Get Out of Bed**
The internal clock that governs many of our body's functions roughly follows the light/dark cycle. Getting up with the sun helps keep your digestive, cardiovascular and other systems in sync and helps prevent unnecessary grogginess.

**8:00 a.m.**
**Eat Breakfast**
Eating within an hour or two of waking makes you less hungry later. Studies show people who eat a big breakfast consume less food throughout the day (so don't waste this opportunity with a handful of Munchkins).

**10:00 a.m.**
**Tackle That Big Project**
By late morning, your mental faculties hit a peak that won't be repeated until late afternoon. Take advantage of increased clarity by confronting the day's toughest challenges.

**1:00 p.m.**
**Drink Coffee**
Most people drink their cup of joe in the a.m., but caffeine's short-lived energy boost is better used to power through the afternoon's fatigue. If you can't grab a nap, grab a venti. Plus, caffeine helps ward off the afternoon's descent into dry eyes by stimulating tears.

# Your Best Day Ever

**A** PANEL OF EXPERTS on humans' internal clocks, including Dr. Stuart Brody, founding director of the University of California at San Diego's Center for Chronobiology, helps you find your ideal tempo. Most researchers assume a day from 7:00 a.m. to 11:00 p.m., but the chart is still useful to early birds and night owls: Add or subtract however many hours your wake-up time is ahead or behind.

**3:30 p.m.**
**Play a Sport**
If you're looking to crush your competition, try scheduling sports in the late afternoon. Your reaction time is at an all-day high, and your coordination hasn't started deteriorating yet, so you'll be at your best.

**6:00 p.m.**
**Eat Dinner**
Having your last big meal of the day at least four hours before sleep helps with digestion and can prevent problems like acid reflux. Eating early also gives you a chance to burn more calories.

**7:00 p.m.**
**Take a Walk**
At the end of the day, people often feel mentally exhausted from juggling multiple tasks and responsibilities. Resist the urge to burn through a season of *Scandal* on Netflix, and instead take a stroll through the neighborhood. Light physical activity will leave you feeling mentally refreshed.

**9:00 p.m.**
**Get a Novel Idea**
Your mind and body are winding down for the day, and those lowered inhibitions can help you stumble upon the idea for the next *The Great Gatsby*. Or at least the next *Fifty Shades of Grey*.

**11 p.m.**

**5:00 p.m.**
**Lift Weights**
In the late afternoon to early evening, your muscles and cardiovascular system will both be operating at peak performance. Hit the gym and start breaking some personal records.

**6:30 p.m.**
**Enjoy a Glass of Wine**
It's better to imbibe in the early evening and not in the wee hours of the morning. Your body, including your liver, is better at processing alcohol at dusk. An 8-ounce serving of alcohol at midnight can have up to three times the intoxicating effect as at 6:00 p.m.

**7:30 p.m.**
**Have a Passionate Conversation**
If you need to tell your spouse about that Porsche you bought at lunch or how their favorite T-shirt from college resembles a rag better used to clean a septic tank, now's the time to do so. Your mental skills are still relatively sharp, and your low blood pressure minimizes your chance of dying from a rage-induced heart attack.

**11:00 p.m.**
**Go to Sleep**
Most people feel sleepy 16 hours after waking up, and the brain has been secreting the hormone melatonin for a few hours now, telling the body it's time to end the day and hit the hay.

THE ULTIMATE HOLISTIC HANDBOOK FOR BEGINNERS

FITNESS

# Notes

# Notes

# A Happier You

Whether at home or on the go,
find fulfillment in life by surrounding
yourself with the things that spark joy
and bring you peace of mind.

# Grace Under (Blood) Pressure

Everything you need to know about hypertension—and what you can do to reach the right blood pressure.

## 7 STEPS TO KEEPING YOUR BLOOD PRESSURE IN CHECK

ARTERIES DISPERSE blood from your heart to every single body part. Blood pressure is the measure of how well all that blood can travel through them. Blood pressure is expressed as a fraction because it represents two separate pressures. The first is systolic pressure, which is the pressure of the blood against the artery walls when the heart beats. After the slash comes the diastolic pressure, which is the pressure between beats. Too much pressure makes artery walls thicken to withstand it. Thicker walls mean less room inside for blood to pass—which increases the pressure yet again. Eventually, the walls give in and burst, or the arteries close up. Either shunts the precious blood supply.

A blood pressure reading of around 120/80 or lower is normal. Pre-hypertension is what doctors call blood pressure higher than 120/80. Having hypertension is more common for people over the age of 50, and two-thirds of people over 65 have it. If blood pressures above 140/90 are ignored, hypertension can open the door to its bigger, badder cohorts—including stroke, heart attack, congestive heart failure, kidney damage and blindness. Here's what to do to make sure those pathways can keep the blood pumping safely.

**1 SLASH THE SALT**
Salt makes your kidneys hold on to water, and that extra fluid puts more pressure on the artery walls. Limit sodium to 2,300 mg a day or less—1,500 mg a day if you are 51 or older, or if you already have hypertension.

**2 WATCH YOUR MIDDLE**
Carrying extra weight, particularly around the midsection, increases blood pressure. Men are at risk if their waist measurement is greater than 40 inches. Women are at risk if their waist measurement is greater than 35 inches.

**3 MOVE MORE**
Regular exercise—at least 30 to 60 minutes most days of the week, according to the Mayo Clinic—can lower your blood pressure readings by four to nine units.

**4 GO BANANAS**
Potassium can help counteract the negative effects of sodium on blood pressure. Consider adding significant sources of potassium—such as spinach—to your diet.

**5 TIPPLE (A LITTLE)**
An alcoholic drink a day can lower your blood pressure numbers by two to four units, according to the Mayo Clinic, but any more

**Exercise that strengthens your heart, such as spinning, is a solid investment of time and energy.**

than that may actually raise blood pressure in those over 65. If you're under 65, stick to two drinks or less. (If you're not already a drinker, doctors don't advise starting.)

### ⑥ DROP THE SMOKES
Smoking can increase your numbers by 10 up to half an hour after you light up.

### ⑦ CALM DOWN
Stress can boost blood pressure temporarily. Simmer down for success.

# IN THE BLOOD
Giving you the lowdown on the life-giving liquid

## Gets around
A red blood cell makes about 250,000 trips around the circulatory system before dying. In men, 47 percent of blood is made up of red blood cells, and, in females, red blood cells make up 42 percent. The ratio of red blood cells to total blood amount is known as the "hematocrit." Another ingredient of your blood, plasma, is made up of 90 percent water and contains hundreds of different molecules, each helping with absorption, clotting and overall blood health.

## Vessel of choice
All of your body's blood vessels, laid end-to-end, would measure 60,000 miles. Your heart pumps blood to almost every one of your body's 75 trillion cells. Only your eyes' corneas receive no supply of blood.

## Keep it clear
When cholesterol goes unchecked, it can cause plaque buildup in your arteries, impeding blood flow from the heart to the rest of the body. When blockage becomes severe, it can result in a heart attack, also called a myocardial infarction.

THE ULTIMATE HOLISTIC HANDBOOK FOR BEGINNERS

# All-Natural Beauty Tips

Avoid the chemicals in the makeup aisle with these easy, at-home DIY beauty remedies.

### SPICES AND OIL FOR GLOWING SKIN
Mix equal parts saffron, sandalwood oil and turmeric with a tablespoon of either yogurt or milk and combine to make a paste.

### SAFFRON
One of the rarest, most expensive spices in the world. In India, it is considered the spice of the gods—a symbol of good luck, holiness and purity. As part of your at-home remedy, it is a natural skin toner.

### SANDALWOOD
A natural astringent and antiseptic, which makes it perfect for battling blemishes. As an added plus, it smells great!

### TURMERIC
Particularly healing if you're sick with a stomach infection. Indian doctors will give you turmeric with milk because it's a natural antibiotic. It works the same way with the skin; if you get a cut, just dab a little turmeric on it and it will heal faster. When you apply the solution on your skin it will give off a pleasant aroma and leave a nice golden color. Rinse off after a few minutes, repeat the process up to three times a week.

### OLIVE OIL
Rubbing virgin olive oil on the face and body after sun exposure can help combat skin cancer. The vitamin E and other antioxidants in virgin olive oil help "mop up" and neutralize some of the free radicals created from UV rays. It's also a great all-natural moisturizer!

### HOMEMADE CONDITIONER
Blend together 1 cup water (boiled or distilled), 1 tsp coconut oil (melted), and ½ tsp Guar gum. This recipe should last about a month. Take a heaping tablespoon (about what you can fit on two fingertips) and apply

### COCONUT OIL
With its composition of medium chain fatty acids, coconut oil is extremely effective at keeping skin healthy and free from dryness and wrinkles. It can also be used to hydrate hair due to its ability to penetrate deep into the hair shaft and scalp. The oil acts from deep within to ensure conditioning and moisturizing effects are long-lasting.

### ALOE VERA FOR DRY SKIN
Store-bought moisturizing creams for dry skin can contain a myriad of unnatural ingredients. Instead of contaminating your body with these chemicals, simply cut the leaves of the aloe vera plant, collect the gel and apply it to your skin. Aloe vera also works as a great treatment for sunburns

### HENNA FOR HAIR DYE
Most synthetic hair dye products contain chemicals called aromatic amines that have been linked to cancer. Combine ½ cup henna with a teaspoon each of sesame oil and curry leaves. Add into a mix of curd, lemon juice and tea to achieve the shade that you desire. More tea will lead to a darker color, while more lemon juice will give you a brighter shade.

### NATURAL DEODORANT STICK
Rather than a chemical-heavy deodorant full of unnatural ingredients, you can try an all-natural deodorant, such as Rose + Vanilla

**Coconut oil also makes a great substitute for vegetable oil in most recipes.**

from Schmidt's. Ingredients include arrowroot powder, coconut oil, candelilla wax, shea butter, baking soda, fractionated coconut oil, jojoba seed oil and vitamin E.

### TEA TREE OIL
Tea tree oil is a great natural product that fights breakouts, redness and skin inflammation. It's perfect to use a few drops in at-home remedies for acne.

### APPLE CIDER VINEGAR
Apple cider vinegar helps kill pathogens, clear skin problems caused by gut issues, cleanse skin and fight acne. Use a few drops on your skin or drink a shot.

# Your Pocket Naturalist

Since the advent of the app revolution, it has never been easier to implement and maintain a healthy lifestyle.

### SHOPWELL
Sticking to a healthy eating plan just became easier with ShopWell. Tell the app what your fitness or diet goals are, and it'll tell you the right food to buy. Add your height, weight, age and allergies, and then it will score every food you eat based on how healthy it is for you. The app also suggests new foods to try that fit with your lifestyle. *Free, iOS and Android*

### MEDITATION STUDIO
Meditate anytime and anywhere with the Meditation Studio app. You can learn the basics of meditation (or do a deep dive) with more than 700 guided meditations, which means this app can also help relieve stress, improve your sleep quality and boost your confidence. Filter meditations by duration, type or teacher. *Free with option to upgrade, iOS and $3.99, Android*

### SLEEP CYCLE: SMART ALARM CLOCK
Getting quality shut-eye goes a long way. With the Sleep Cycle: Smart Alarm Clock app, you can track your sleep patterns with in-depth statistics and still wake up right on time to start your day. *Free with in-app purchases, iOS and Android*

### COUCH-TO-5K
Couch potatoes can now become 5K completists with this app that takes beginners and slowly progresses their walk-to-run-to-rest ratio to turn a novice runner into an experienced road warrior

in just eight weeks. Each week, you are required to run a little more and walk a little less, until you are running 20 minutes straight with more ease and comfort than the week before. *$2.99, iOS and Android*

### YOGA STUDIO
Thanks to this expansive app you can carry an entire ashram in your pocket. Yoga Studio includes 65 classes for all different levels (beginner, intermediate or advanced), durations (15, 30 or 60 minutes) and focuses (strength, flexibility, relaxation, balance or combination), so it's simple to find the perfect class for you. All classes include full HD video and teacher commentary, which makes the classes easy to follow, even for beginners. Now if you could only find a way to stuff a mat in your purse. *Free with in-app purchases, iOS and Android*

### FOODUCATE
Fooducate helps users become fluent in the nutrition information on food labels. This app lets you either scan the barcode of a product or type in its name to analyze its total calories, fat, sodium and other ingredients. It also scores the food for healthiness and might just uncover a few fatty secrets about that lunch salad. *Free with in-app purchases, iOS and Android*

### HELLOFRESH
Now you can finish all your errands and still have time to cook well-balanced, healthy meals. This app delivers portioned ingredients straight to your door, starting at less than $10 per meal. Along with providing the potential allergens with every recipe, each dish is grouped with holistic nutritional information including the amount of calories, fats, carbohydrates, protein, fiber and sodium. *Free with pay subscription service, iOS and Android*

# A More Natural Routine

**By introducing a mindful approach to your daily tasks, you'll help melt away your stress.**

### MORNING

**1** Before you get out of bed, take three deep, meditative breaths. Quiet your mind and let yourself focus. Notice the sounds and light in the room and how your body feels.

**2** Hydrate before your morning coffee. When you wake up after a good night's sleep, your body will be dehydrated. Drink an entire cup of water before you reach for your caffeine fix. When you move on to your morning beverage of choice, pay attention to its preparation. Don't multitask while you drink—no screens, no to-do lists, no agendas. Prepare and sip your drink, and focus on being fully present.

**3** Rather than going directly to a screen as you get going in the morning, step outside for a few minutes and take in some nature. Notice the different sounds, smells and sights. Appreciating your environment will help you feel more grounded and connected.

**4** Take 10 minutes at the start of your work day, whether it be in your car or at your desk, to engage in a short mindfulness practice. Relax your body while sitting with good posture and your eyes closed, and simply focus on your breathing. When you feel your attention drifting, refocus on your breath.

If the need to procrastinate hits, the best thing to do is face it head on: Ask yourself why you're putting off the task at hand—and be honest.

This will allow you to start your work day with a quiet and relaxed mind, rather than feeling frazzled and rushed after your commute.

## AFTERNOON

**1** Block out time in your schedule to take a break for lunch every day. Don't work through lunch and eat at your desk—instead, invite colleagues to join you or take a break and sit outside.

**2** After lunch, set an alarm on your phone for every hour. Whenever it goes off, do a single minute of deep-breathing. This will help your focus and allow you to feel present for the rest of your day, even as you begin to tire and look forward to getting home.

## EVENING

**1** When you walk through your front door, imagine yourself shedding the worries and anxieties of your day. Don't carry the workday into the house with you. Instead, focus on entering the door without any office-related worries.

**2** Focus on different sensations when you eat dinner. How was the food prepared? What are the different scents in your kitchen? How does the food taste? Chew slowly and take a moment to reflect on both the taste as well as the act of eating.

**3** Take at least five minutes to do nothing but reflect—no phone, no TV, no newspaper. Don't even try to meditate. Just sit and reflect on your day. Embrace any frustration with the day and focus on moving through it, rather than letting any resentment build.

**4** One hour before you go to sleep, dim the lights and put away any screens. This will help your body begin to relax as you prepare to go to sleep and is a great time to start a new reading regimen.

# The Essential Guide to Essential Oils

A detailed primer on some of nature's most useful ingredients.

AS INTEREST IN alternative remedies grows among those looking for less synthetics in their lives, so does the popularity of essential oils. These oils are naturally occurring and are extracted from the roots, leaves, seeds or blossoms of plants. For thousands of years, they have been applied topically, inhaled or ingested for both physical and emotional healing. Ancient Egypt, China, Greece and all the countries to which their hegemonies extended used essential oils for therapeutic purposes as well as religious and ritualistic ones. For these cultures, the properties of essential oils were nothing short of magical, but modern science is finally beginning to unlock their secrets.

In the early 20th century, after applying lavender to a burn, French chemist René-Maurice Gattefossé began to study the chemical properties of essential oils and invented the term aromatherapy. But, it wouldn't be until the 1980s that aromatherapy would become popular in the United States. According to a study by Research and Markets, the U.S. essential oil market is projected to hit $7.34 billion by 2024 with the aromatherapy sector making up more than 25 percent of the revenue share.

Just like the ingredients themselves haven't changed much in the centuries since they were discovered and developed, neither have the applications. Any of the following "starter kit" of essential oils can be added to a bath, used in aromatherapy, added to a lotion and applied topically or used as a cold compress by adding a few drops of oil to a rag saturated with icy water.

## LAVENDER
If you only have one essential oil on hand, lavender is a good choice. It is known for its calming properties and is used to help relieve stress and anxiety and improve insomnia. It also has healing properties. It can be used to treat wounds, burns and skin disorders such as eczema. Additionally, it can be used to help alleviate headaches. Research has found that lavender, when applied topically or used as part of an aromatherapy regimen, also helps to increase pain tolerance.

## CLARY SAGE
The word clary is derived from the Latin word clarus, meaning clear. Clary sage oil has been used in medicine since ancient Egypt, but usage took off in the medieval period when it was employed to treat vision issues. Clary sage oil is often utilized to regulate hormones; it can be used to help assuage symptoms of premenstrual syndrome and menopause because it contains estrogen compounds. In a 2014 study, it was shown breathing diffused clary sage helped ease the subjects' depression.

## TEA TREE
The aboriginal people of Australia have long used tea tree oil as medicine for injuries. It can kill some bacteria, viruses and fungi upon

contact. Today, tea tree oil is often used to treat cuts and insect bites, and according to the National Center for Complementary and Integrative Health research has shown the oil is helpful for acne, nail fungus and athlete's foot.

## PATCHOULI

Patchouli is the essential oil that gets better with age. As it gets older, the oil's color and viscosity deepen, and the fragrance gets richer. It's a tool often used to fight skin and hair problems such as dandruff, oily scalp, sunburn, acne and eczema. It's sometimes utilized to combat fungal infections, inflammation and colds. It also has mental benefits, as it can have a relaxing, sedative effect.

## PEPPERMINT

You're probably using peppermint already in your toothpaste, your mouthwash or maybe your gum. But peppermint does more than combat bad breath and other odors. It's used to increase focus and energy, soothe headaches and treat nausea. Additionally, studies have shown that peppermint oil might be helpful in improving symptoms associated with irritable bowel syndrome.

## FRANKINCENSE

Perhaps best known as one of three gifts brought to Jesus of Nazareth at the nativity, frankincense has been valued for centuries for its medicinal properties. It can be used to soothe boils and ingrown hairs as well as smooth wrinkles and heal acne scars, age spots and sun damage. It is also utilized to boost immunity, fight infections, reduce inflammation and can combat bad breath, mouth sores and toothaches.

## CHAMOMILE

There are two main types of chamomile oil: Roman chamomile and German chamomile. The plants these oils are derived from are different species, but the oils are used to treat the same issues. You might be familiar with the relaxing and sedating properties of chamomile tea, and chamomile oil can have the same effect. The oil is also helpful for a variety of ailments, including allergies, skin irritation, arthritis, nausea, vomiting, heartburn and gas.

## SANDALWOOD

Ancient Egyptians imported the wood from sandalwood trees and used it for embalming as well as ritual burning. The wood and its oil are also important to three main world religions: Hinduism, Buddhism and Islam. Like other essential oils, sandalwood is often used as a skin care tool. It can also help increase focus, control anxiety and heal wounds. Some research has shown that sandalwood might even help fight skin cancer.

**A diffuser is a great way to passively enjoy the benefits of essential oils.**

# A Happier Home

### Seven simple, feng shui-inspired hacks to turn your house into a sanctuary of calm.

FOR THOUSANDS of years, people have sought to bring balance and order to their lives by following the principles of feng shui. More than just an organizational tool, feng shui (which translates to "water-wind") reminds us to consider the energy we welcome into our homes. Numerous elements of your humble abode can have a positive or negative affect on this flow of energy, which in turn can impact your quality of life.

While traditional feng shui draws on Taoist philosophy and Chinese cultural elements, you don't have to be a Buddhist to embrace these basic feng shui essentials, which will immediately start reframing your home in a whole-new light. This ancient approach imbues commonsense cleaning advice with intention and mindfulness. Why not boost your mood, lower your stress, improve your focus and more by implementing the techniques below?

### ❶ CLEAR THE CLUTTER

Get started on your feng shui journey by identifying sources of clutter in your home. Imagine where you stack the books you've been meaning to put back on the shelf, or the place where your mail piles up in the kitchen. Wherever your disordered disaster lives, mess is distracting and stressful to look at; a thing out of place is a job left undone, which can create anxiety if you're the one doing the cleaning. In 2011, researchers at Princeton University found clutter can overwhelm your visual cortex, hindering your ability to focus and making it harder for you to power through your to-do list. But don't let clutter get you down: Pick a room and take a few minutes to put your books away, gather loose papers and find a home for whatever sticks out. Tackle one job at a time and you'll find you've tidied up your place faster than you can say Marie Kondo.

### ❷ CHECK THE FLOW

Take a step back and look at your home, room by room, as a whole. Clear any remaining clutter around your doors or windows. When you can reach what you need when you need it, when you can move freely throughout your space, when things feel relatively light and airy, you'll know you've established a good flow of positive energy. Guide the good vibes through your home with feng shui and let your space work toward your greatest good.

### ❸ LET THE LIGHT IN

Light sets the mood and changes the tone of a room in a flash. Consider your lighting: Does your living room get enough natural light, or does it feel more like a cave? When you maximize the natural light in your house, you can boost your mood and even your immune system. Use mirrors (a feng shui staple) to catch light and movement, drawing even more good energy into your space. Depending on what you do in each room, determine whether the lighting helps or hinders you. Bright LED bulbs on your bedside table could be keeping you from falling asleep quickly. Swap direct lighting, like spotlights, for ambient lighting by placing lamps with warm-colored shades in the corners of your room.

### 4) ADD SOME COLOR

The psychological benefits of colors are endless. Look at your walls, your rugs and any large objects in your room—what color(s) are they? A bright lime green paint job in the bedroom might come off like a shot of caffeine in a space where you're trying to relax, but in your entryway could make for a welcome jolt of energy as you head out in the morning. In the rooms where you go to unwind, update your accent colors to soothing, light or cozy tones like light blues, neutrals or other pastels. Save bolder colors for the kitchen, office or wherever you like to get creative for an added spark. Aside from piquing your interest or calming frazzled nerves, color can also make a room look smaller or larger depending on the hue. Experiment with color and pay close attention to how your lighting affects your space to make the most of every room.

### 5) KEEP IT COMFY

Whether you're drawn to the sleek lines of mid-century modern furniture or have a few eclectic pieces you've picked up over the years, your furnishings also represent the support you need. Whatever your setup, the furniture in your home should be comfortable, welcoming and sturdy. Those creaky, stained folding chairs you saved from your college days aren't doing you any favors. If your pieces look outdated, worn or otherwise tired, let them go. It's easy to imbue items with emotional significance, but by purging objects that no longer serve us well, we make room for fresh new memories (and new furniture you can be proud of).

### 6) LOVE YOUR BED

We spend about a third of our lives sleeping. That's some serious bed bonding time. Your bed is where you spend the most time at home, and in feng shui it represents, well, you. Make sure your mattress, sheets, pillows and headboard are all clean, in good shape, supportive and comfortable. If you've accumulated mess under your bed, pitch that clutter ASAP to minimize the stress in the literal home of your dreams. Most importantly, your mother was right: Make your bed every morning. Doing this simple task sets you up for a positive, job-tackling momentum to face the day. Give your bed the space it deserves and get some much-needed rest in return.

### 7) FIND YOUR FAVORITES

Maybe you own an enviable collection of vintage vinyl, you're partial to pineapples or you love the look of old, hand-drawn maps. Whatever your passion, show off the items that speak to you. The easiest way to punch up the positive energy in your home is to prominently feature objects that spark joy. Without falling back into clutter, designate a space where you can showcase your hobbies, souvenirs from your travels or whatever you prize most. Decorate your place with your favorite things and your little sanctuary will start to feel like heaven.

A HAPPIER YOU

# Just Breathe

One thing all mindfulness experts tend to agree on is the importance of breath in their attempts to be present. These six techniques can help even the most inexperienced mindfulness seekers find a moment of peace.

### 1 THE "BELLOWS BREATH"
Also known as the stimulating breath, this exercise is meant to focus your mind on the action rather than the length of your breath and is said to energize as well as produce a mindful state. It is performed by inhaling and exhaling deeply and rapidly through the nose while leaving the mouth relaxed. A good aim is for three in-and-out cycles per second, and the exercise should not extend past 10 or 15 seconds.

### 2 ABDOMINAL BREATHING
Able to immediately slow the heart rate and calm the mind and body, breathing deeply with one hand on the chest, directly into the diaphragm (by bending the knees, placing one hand on the chest and one over the stomach and breathing deeply in through the nose so the stomach inflates) can be a deceptively difficult technique for novices. Aiming for six to 10 of these breaths in a row is a great way to start.

### 3 THE "4-7-8" EXERCISE
The numbers in the name of this exercise are supposed to be the ideal ratio for the counts involved in a complete breath, It is one of the most surefire ways to focus on nothing but the breath and its count because it keeps your mind occupied with the ratio at all times. Beginning with an emptying exhale, inhale through your nose for a count of four, hold your breath for a count of seven and exhale for a count of eight. Repeat.

### 4 COUNTING
The simplest and perhaps most practiced form of breath exercise is the simple counting of breaths. Each time you exhale, add a count. Use groups of five or simply keep counting up.

### 5 SAMA VRITTI OR "EQUAL BREATHING"
Based on the idea that a balanced or symmetrical approach is good for the body and soul, equal breathing is a technique in which the inhalation and exhalation are meant to be exactly the same length. By focusing on keeping the two identical, we can often attain a mindful state usually associated with formal meditation.

### 6 NADI SHODHANA OR "ALTERNATE NOSTRIL BREATHING"
Made famous and utilized most often by practitioners of yoga, the technique of guiding air through one nostril at a time, inhaling through the left and exhaling through the right. Yogis claim that this technique offers them as much energy as a cup of coffee and is a perfect exercise for a stressful time like a deadline.

# Notes

## Special Section
# Nature's Remedies

From soothing frazzled nerves to healing aches and pains, this handy herbal index will show you how to make the most of the medicine growing right in your backyard.

### WHEN IN DOUBT, GOOGLE IT
Even herbal experts can agree that a few minutes of online research—checking the color, leaves, etc.—will help you know for sure whether that plant you plucked won't put you six feet under.

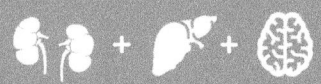

# Agrimony

**benefits**

## quick facts

- A highly tannic herb, agrimony will have a familiar feeling for red wine drinkers if made into an infusion. Take 1 to 2 teaspoons of agrimony per cup of tea, steeping 8–10 minutes.

- Though you should consult with your doctor before doing so, taking a supplement of agrimony orally has been shown to increase the effectiveness of certain medications.

- Do you find yourself holding your breath when in physical pain? This reflex can help ease immediate responses and dull discomfort, but if done excessively can prevent enough oxygen from getting where it needs to be in the body. Agrimony can help you relax and let the central nervous system compensate by sending blood—and therefore oxygen—to restricted spaces.

THIS MEMBER of the Rosaceae family has a pleasing and delicate scent and is a powerful cleanser of the filter organs such as the liver and kidneys. A natural astringent, diuretic and relaxant, agrimony can be fashioned into a somewhat bitter tonic that can ease various kinds of pain, especially if the discomfort happens to be caused by kidney or bladder stones. In Chinese traditional medicine, the liver is supposed to be responsible for housing a person's anger, and agrimony is the time-tested method of cleansing emotional stress from the body. As a supplement used to treat fear and anxiety, the strong herb can help those who worry excessively about work, relationships, money or other existentialisms.

Agrimony can be recognized in the wild by its multiple pinnate leaves with larger examples (6"-8") closer to the base and 3" leaves at the top. Small yellow flowers with five oval-shaped and narrow petals are supported by skinny spikes. You may find that the plant grows best in soil lightened with a little bit of sand and takes well to narrow nooks with full sunlight.

**Agrimony may be able to moderate the glucose and insulin in your body, a possible step toward curing diabetes.**

SPECIAL SECTION

**SILICIC ACID** has been shown to promote hair and nail growth and is found in agrimony.

THE ULTIMATE HOLISTIC HANDBOOK FOR BEGINNERS 85

# Balsam Fir

**benefits**

## quick facts

- Using 1 tablespoon of leaves and twigs per cup of tea and steeping covered for 8-10 minutes can produce a powerful infusion for throat and respiratory ailments.

- A balsam salve can go directly onto the skin and can help with pain from burns, wounds, toothaches, muscle strains and other topical complaints. Nursing mothers, for example, might find such a salve particularly soothing.

- Some herbal practitioners swear by balsam fir as a valuable tool in the fight to quit smoking. The plant soothes the side effects of nicotine withdrawal such as irritability, constipation and trouble sleeping.

- The inner bark of the balsam fir is a valuable cure for gastrointestinal inflammation, especially if caused by cystitis.

YOU MIGHT recognize this herbal powerhouse as your friendly neighborhood Christmas tree, but don't let the festivity fool you. When it comes to herbal healing, this plant is all business. An evergreen conifer whose needles have silvery undersides and whose bark is covered in a layer of pitch, balsam fir can also lend every part of itself to herbal medicine. High in vitamin A, calcium and iron, balsam fir infusions, tinctures and salves can work wonders on the bladder, lungs and skin.

You can tell the balsam fir apart from other coniferous varieties by its ¾"-1 ½" blunt needles and purplish pinecones that are never intact when they reach the forest floor thanks to the fact that they break open when mature. If you're growing your own from a seed, the best time to plant is in early spring with the aid of a greenhouse. If you're foraging for your balsam fir, be careful to thoroughly check and adhere to your local government guidelines on trimming, which will likely prohibit taking from the main branches and limit your trimmings by size.

**The balsam fir was first described as an independent species in 1768.**

SPECIAL SECTION

**STICK TO IT**
Balsam fir resin is an adhesive used in optical glass and slides.

THE ULTIMATE HOLISTIC HANDBOOK FOR BEGINNERS  87

SPECIAL SECTION

## holy basil

Also commonly known as tulsi, holy basil is native to India and has been in consistent use there for three millennia. For a tonic to restore energy and vigor, you can use holy basil in a tincture with 80-proof alcohol. Two or three times a day, take a teaspoon of the tincture orally to regenerate after injury or illness or to put some needed pep in your step.

# Basil

**benefits**

## quick facts

- You can make a quick basil tea for stress headaches with either fresh herbs from your garden or dried basil that has been stored. Take one part basil leaf, one part lemon balm leaf and ¼ part chamomile or lavender and infuse for 15 minutes before straining, then drink warm, not as hot as regular tea.

- Basil poultices are one of the oldest cures in the world. Simply mash (or, if you're feeling particularly traditional, chew) some leaves until they're soft and place them directly on a sting or bite and leave it on for 15 minutes.

- Your plants will thrive and produce more leaves for your kitchen and medicine chest if you remember to fertilize throughout the season. Fish emulsions work particularly well.

*BASILUCUM*, the technical species name for this common herb and best friend of Italian food, comes from a Greek root meaning "royal herb." It's a fitting name, given the first medications made with the staple of herbal gardens everywhere were created for kings. Both the leaves and the flowers are valued in the medicine cabinet (the leaves don't do too badly in the kitchen, either). Able to ease gas and cramps as well as calm other stomach maladies, basil also has the benefit of being one of the easiest herbs to cultivate in a home garden.

Sensitive to cold weather, basil can be planted as soon as temperatures break 50 degrees Fahrenheit. Plants should be monitored and trimmed so they're at least 7" apart to make sure each one gets full sun. Harvesting couldn't be easier. Simply pick off leaves as they grow throughout the season with an eye toward giving the leaves still on the plant increased exposure to the sun. One of the oldest and most trusted herbs in the world, basil has no known side effects and is edible in its raw form as well as in prepared medicine and can be used as a poultice, for its oil, in tinctures and other applications.

## Basil is rich in vitamins A, B6 and C, as well as being an excellent source of magnesium and iron.

# Blackberry

### benefits

### quick facts

- Blackberry leaf is valued for its remarkable astringency, but this benefit could backfire if the herbal remedy is used too much. It is so good at controlling blood flow that some women have experienced an inhibition of menses.

- A perennial plant that takes best to acidic, slightly sandy soil, blackberry will thrive if given access to plenty of sunlight. But make sure to give them their own room to grow, otherwise they can easily take over your whole garden.

- More spiritual herbalists credit blackberry with having an effect on the user's ability to directly focus their will, giving them more control over their actions.

**WHOLE FOOD** Eat whole fresh berries for maximum antioxidants.

ALSO KNOWN AS brambleberry for the procumbent manner in which its bushes grow, blackberry is more than just a delicious filling for your favorite old-timey desserts.

It's also a natural remedy powerhouse thanks to its soothing effects on the gastrointestinal tract, specifically against what some traditionalists might call "damp stomach," i.e. a buildup of mucus in the stomach causing nausea, food stagnation or loose bowels. A powerful natural astringent, blackberry is a tummy cure-all that's hard to beat for "spoonful of sugar" value. No additives are needed to make this medicine go down.

In addition to a blackberry leaf infusion's proven power against complaints of the GI tract, throat pain can be tackled without going for heavily medicated cough syrups. A simple syrup made with blackberry is a cure that has been in use in some cultures for centuries. Though even traditional practitioners might overlook blackberry because it is so readily available and popular as a food—it can hide in plain sight—the plant is undergoing a renaissance as an herbal cure.

Historically, the blackberry leaf was used by the Oneida people of the northeast U.S. and Great Lakes to boost immunity against new diseases brought to the North American continent by white settlers. These tribes would fortify their gastrointestinal tracts against the strange maladies the settlers and their food and drink could present, letting blackberry help them deal with whatever new germs might show up during this often contentious cultural exchange.

SPECIAL SECTION

SPECIAL SECTION

**IDENTIFIER
8-12
number of petals on a bloodroot flower**

In March and April, bloodroot is in peak flower.

# Bloodroot

## benefits

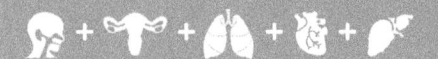

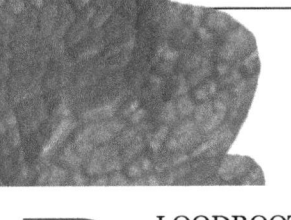

BLOODROOT, which gets its name from the deep red color of its tendrilous roots, is one of the most powerful tools in the arsenal of herbal healers thanks to its acute ability to help women in need of escharotic—scab-making—medication for cervical dysplasia. This condition, which refers to abnormal pre-cancerous and perhaps cancerous growths on the cervix, is tested for at yearly gynecological checkups and if detected early can be treated with ease before it causes any long-term damage. Despite its traditional status and popularity among herbalists, bloodroot is also so undeniably effective that it is a staple in pharmaceutical treatments for cervical dysplasia as well as being the go-to traditional remedy.

In addition to its benefits to the reproductive system, bloodroot can be used as a stimulant, speeding up central nervous system function and promoting increased blood flow. Helping to "warm" the organs, bloodroot improves function in the filtering organs like the liver as well as making sure the lungs, heart and reproductive system get their optimum amount of circulation. However, not be used by children, pregnant women or new mothers who are breastfeeding due to the alkaloids present. If used too much, these same alkaloids can eventuate toxic buildup, so don't overdo the use of this valuable restorative.

## quick facts

- Bloodroot rhizomes can be used as a decoction, tincture or syrup to promote internal health. Just take some bloodroot once a day (1 teaspoon in a cup of tea, a teaspoon of syrup or 5–10 drops of a tincture).

- In addition to its internal benefits, bloodroot is one of the few herbs that can also benefit the sinuses when used as a snuff. Take a pinch of ground root for sinus headaches or infections.

- Bloodroot is listed as endangered in some areas, so be sure you adhere to the local guidelines regarding harvesting before you refill your medicine cabinet.

### ...in a name
The darkened color of this plant's root system is appropriate given how virile the plant can prove to be. Bloodroot self-seeds and will slowly but surely build up a sizeable colony.

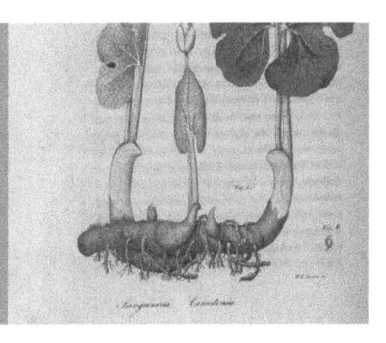

# Boneset

**benefits**

## quick facts

- Depending on your region, you might also hear boneset referred to as thoroughwort, crosswort, Indian sage or feverwort.

- Boneset is high in vitamin D1, which is valuable because many Americans suffer from a vitamin D deficiency.

- Boneset grows best in low, open spaces, thriving particularly well in swampland. For home growers, any soil will do for this plant—it's not picky. Just make sure it gets full sunlight.

DESPITE ITS name, this member of the family Asteraceae is not traditionally used to help heal fractures, and no study has ever proven it can (though some herbalists have used boneset poultices in this context and claim moderate success). But that doesn't mean the herb is useless in the medicine chest. In fact, it is a powerful aid in breaking fevers and is a specific against the chills and bone aches that often come along with them.

Both the leaves and stems of boneset can be used to make infusions and tinctures that will help draw out the infection causing your fever while acting on the most unpleasant physical effects. To make a healing cup of boneset tea, simply add 1 to 2 teaspoons to your tea before letting it steep for up to 10 minutes. Then take 4 ounces of the infusion every hour to break an active fever. As a preventative, take one to three cups a day.

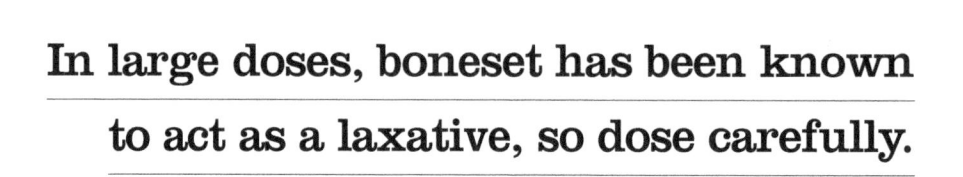

**In large doses, boneset has been known to act as a laxative, so dose carefully.**

SPECIAL SECTION

## particulars
Boneset thrives in partial sun and rich, wet soil, and as an added bonus, livestock find it too bitter to graze on, so your crop will be safe from curious critters.

**THE ULTIMATE HOLISTIC HANDBOOK FOR BEGINNERS 95**

# Calamus

**benefits**

## quick facts

- Though it's an extremely useful herbal medicine, if taken in extremely large doses calamus has been known to become hallucinogenic.

- Its scientific name is *Acorus calamus*, but calamus has also been called flag root, sweet myrtle, sweet sedge, gladdon and vacha.

- When not flowering, calamus can be easily confused with yellow iris—at least by sight. Calamus can be identified by the lemony smell of its oil.

GONE HOARSE? If you're already brewing a piping hot cup of tea, why not take a minute to add a teaspoon of calamus root? The herb known as the best friend of orators and singers might just become your go-to cure for everything that ails your vocal chords, from laryngitis to post-concert voice loss.

Once that calamus decoction goes down, it switches focus from the throat to the stomach, where it helps treat indigestion, flatulence and other GI complaints. Chewing a small piece of calamus root, in fact, is a specific way to battle the reflux condition known as water brash, when thin, watery bile is regurgitated into the mouth. As needed for reflux complaints, some herbalists recommend chewing a teaspoon or two of root.

There is also some evidence that calamus can help improve brain function. In Chinese traditional medicine, similar plants were said to clear the brain of mucus-like blockages, restoring cognitive function and allowing patients who were addled by trauma or illness to become comprehensive in their thought process again.

*A powerful tool for singers, calamus has been in use for more than 2,000 years.*

SPECIAL SECTION

## calamus plant

In some Native American traditions, calamus root was ritually smoked as part of ceremonies as well as used in this fashion as part of herbal treatment.

**THE ULTIMATE HOLISTIC HANDBOOK FOR BEGINNERS 97**

## benefits

# Cayenne

## quick facts

- When handling cayenne directly, those with sensitive skin may find mere contact can create a burning sensation. There's no shame in wearing gloves when working with these peppers. If you don't, be sure to wash your hands after and keep your hands away from your eyes.

- Less is more when using cayenne. Stomach convulsions have been known to occur in those who use too large a dose.

- To make a cayenne rub for treating achy joints, combine ½ cup of olive oil with 1 tablespoon of dried cayenne (either powdered or flaked) with ⅛ cup beeswax. Heat the mixture over a very low flame until it reaches the desired consistency. You can add more beeswax for a harder finished product or more oil for a softer one. Add a few drops of a stimulating essential oil like wintergreen when you remove it from the burner. This will give your finished product a more mellow feeling and cut down on the heat.

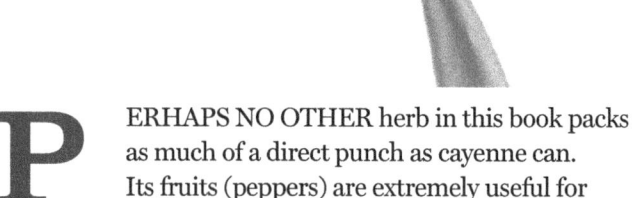

PERHAPS NO OTHER herb in this book packs as much of a direct punch as cayenne can. Its fruits (peppers) are extremely useful for ailments from topical pain to nasal congestion. In fact, you'd be hard-pressed to find a more powerful natural decongestant anywhere. For a quick cold capsule that will keep your sinuses open and airy all winter, combine one part each of echinacea root powder and goldenseal root powder with a half part each of mallow root powder and cayenne powder in a vegetable gelatin cap.

As a member of the "nightshade" family, only the fruits are safe for use: Leaves and stems can be toxic. The main active ingredient in the cayenne pepper, capsaicin—the element that contains all the spiciness—sends endorphins from the brain, leading to natural pain relief and euphoria. Cayenne is even a main ingredient in many over-the-counter creams for painful conditions like arthritis and tennis elbow. Capsaicin also works to stimulate the digestive system by making the mouth water and the stomach produce enzymes in preparation for the spicy natural cure-all's arrival in the GI tract.

But perhaps the most important property of cayenne is one we are still on our way to understanding completely. Studies in the U.S. and India have recently shown what many herbalists have long suspected—cayenne's most powerful medicinal application might be for heart health. Specifically, cayenne appears to help decrease the severity of certain heart conditions as well as lower cholesterol.

**This pepper is named for the capital city of French Guiana.**

SPECIAL SECTION

### hot stuff
One tablespoon (5g) of cayenne pepper contains 44 percent of the recommended daily allowance of vitamin A, as well as 1.4g of fiber.

THE ULTIMATE HOLISTIC HANDBOOK FOR BEGINNERS 99

SPECIAL SECTION

**SPECIES**
Eastern red cedar is the most commonly used.

# Cedar

**benefits**

## quick facts

- Those with lingering, painful and dry coughs should avoid the use of cedar, as it can aggravate this condition. Cedar works best on a wet, phlegmy cough.

- Cedar can also be known as the tree of life or arbor-vitae.

- Cedar has strong stimulating properties that have been known to induce contractions in the gastrointestinal tract and, in women, the uterus. This can trigger menstruation when needed, but for this reason should be avoided while pregnant.

ONE OF THE most ancient natural remedies in the North American traditions, cedar has been used for centuries against tumors and other growths, decongestion of all kinds and even to prolong the life of cancer patients. Leaves and twigs can be collected to create a powerful anti-inflammatory and astringent. When mucus builds up due to an infection like a cold, cedar is especially effective at breaking that mucus up and allowing your sinuses and other passages to clear. Using about a teaspoon in an infusion, let it steep for a full 15 minutes before enjoying the effects.

In lab conditions, it seems to be more and more clear that cedar has the capability to increase the process of phagocytosis, in which harmful cells like bacteria are digested by other cells, neutralizing them. Used both topically and in injections by some practitioners, cedar has been in use since the 19th century in modern western medicine as a cure for colon cancer and certain uterine cancers. And the leaves and twigs from which cures can be made are able to be harvested year round.

In addition to perhaps being one of the puzzle pieces in our fight against cancer, cedar also has a much more everyday use that is no less effective. A tincture of cedar applied topically to warts and some fungal infections twice daily can rid you of these unpleasant conditions.

**According to some spiritualists, cedar was the first kind of tree in creation.**

# Chamomile

**benefits**

## quick facts

- One of the great benefits of chamomile for budding herbalists is it's relatively easy to grow from seed. So when you're ready to move on from cuttings to seeds, chamomile is a great place to start.

- Chamomile has traditionally been known as the "plant's doctor" because it seems to have a rejuvenating and immunizing effect on the plants around it.

- Because the flowers are easy to pick, the most efficient way to harvest them is to use your hand as a rake, allowing flowers to catch between your fingers a few at a time. This will save time as opposed to plucking flowers individually.

CHAMOMILE MIGHT not be the most physically large or imposing plant in your herb garden, but once it's in the medicine chest, this little herb becomes a behemoth. A gentle plant that is easily potable, chamomile has been approved by official authorities of medicine in no less than 26 countries for indigestion, painful muscle spasms, inflammation, tension, headaches, colic and a range of other maladies both topical and infectious.

The volatile oil azulene, large amounts of which are present in chamomile, is a particularly strong anti-inflammatory and pain reliever, making it a valuable tool against arthritis and similar conditions. In fact, studies have shown that taking a cup of chamomile tea in addition to or instead of regular pain medication can allow arthritis sufferers to enjoy restful, painless sleep. In addition, the digestive and nervous systems can benefit from that same cup of sleepytime tea. Or, if you're feeling particularly stressed, chamomile can be added to your bathwater for a relaxing soak and a massage oil to make sure you take care of that stress in short order.

Some people can be allergic to chamomile flowers, so make sure when trying it for the first time you take a very small dose and watch out for warning signs like itchy eyes or ears, scratchy throat or a runny nose. If you exhibit any of these, chamomile is probably not for you.

**Buckingham Palace uses chamomile instead of grass on some of its vast lawns.**

SPECIAL SECTION

**APPLE SCENT**
The Spanish word for chamomile is *manzanilla*, which means little apple.

# Chicory

### benefits

### quick facts

- According to herbalists who partake in flower essence therapy, in which tinctures are made from the flowers of herbal plants, chicory is used to combat possessive or manipulative behaviors and allows for a less selfish outlook.

- Chicory is rich in beta carotene, the nutrient found in carrots that is traditionally thought to help eyesight. It's also a source of vitamins A and K.

- A tincture of chicory taken by the dropperful three times a day is one of the most effective herbal remedies known for gallbladder colic.

YOU'LL BE ABLE to recognize chicory—also known as succory or hindbeh depending on where you hail from—by its blue flowers, whose many petals end in ridges that resemble sporks. But it's the roots you'll want for your medicine chest. You'll be able to find it in open, sunny areas like open fields or the grassy areas along roadsides, with its flowers opening along with the sun and closing around noon.

Acting on the gastrointestinal system, chicory aids in the breakdown of food into its nutrient and waste components and aids the blood in getting those nutrients around the body, which keeps the blood's toxin levels down and gives filtering organs like the liver and kidneys a decreased workload. Acting on the gallbladder, chicory relieves congestion in the organ by opening up the bile ducts.

Chicory can also help those who are trying to cut down on their coffee habit. Making a tea with chicory and roasted dandelions will result in a dark, bitter brew that will remind you of coffee without making you quite so jumpy after your third cup. You'll find that it helps to steep longer than regular tea, however, so let it stand for around 20 minutes.

**Two tablespoons of chicory contains 33 percent of your daily dose of vitamin A.**

SPECIAL SECTION

## allergy prone
Chicory is closely related to plants like ragweed and marigold, which are well-known allergenic plants, so it is entirely possible that an allergic reaction can occur with chicory as well, and those prone to allergies should be tested before using chicory.

**benefits**

# Cowslip

## quick facts

- Cowslip has some whimsical regional names, including fairy cups, key to heaven and horse buckles.

- When used in a tincture, cowslip is taken in higher quantities than most herbs. Take 10–30 drops, depending on your needs, one to three times a day.

- A well-fertilized cow pasture would be able to be identified in early farming communities by the presence of cowslip, and it can be found today in similar open spaces.

RARE IN THAT the flowers, leaves and stems are all able to be used as part of an herbal treatment plan, cowslip can be recognized by its thick clusters of leaves at the bottom of the plant, a thin stalk and clusters of yellow flowers at the top. These constituent parts make up a plant whose herbal calling is to take on stress in all its forms.

Beginning with its most apparent incarnation, everyday mental stress causes the body's tension to increase in proportion with your own anxieties. This means your heart rate jumps, your breathing becomes labored and your brain function can even be altered. Most of us deal with a certain amount of this kind of stress every day, but the danger lies in the decreased immune response all of this extra bodily function is causing. If you are to fall ill when under a particularly stressful yoke, the illness will hit you much harder than it might have if your body's normal responses weren't being hogged by the side effects of your stress. Enter cowslip, which acts on the nervous, respiratory and cardiovascular systems to decrease tension. This makes it particularly useful for children who have undergone recent stress, but is also invaluable to ease the strain that everyday stress can put on the body.

A useful offshoot of cowslip's tension relief properties is that it is also effective against many kinds of headaches, including tension headaches and migraines. Many herbalists also like to make a wine with cowslip that is a particularly calming pre-bedtime tot and effective against insomnia.

**Cowslip will flower between April and May in nutrient-rich soil.**

SPECIAL SECTION

## May day
Because in some parts of the world cowslip is a traditional flower to pick for May Day celebrations, it can be on decline or even endangered, so be sure to verify the status of the plant in your area.

THE ULTIMATE HOLISTIC HANDBOOK FOR BEGINNERS

## benefits

# Dandelion

### quick facts

- Dandelion stems contain a milky latex that, if applied to warts, can heal them after about 10 days.

- To make a simple Horta, or dandelion green salad, sauté along with other wild greens and drizzle with olive oil and lemon juice. You can also toss in a little feta cheese for another authentic Greek addition, but if you're using Horta as a liver tonic, eat a quarter cup of plain salad three times a day.

- Dandelion roots are best harvested in late fall before they get woody and bitter.

TO MANY PEOPLE in the world, dandelions are viewed as a simple pest. But to others, they're both a delicious leafy green and a valuable source of natural medicine. In any case, the war against dandelions being waged in many parts of America doesn't seem to be working. If dandelions are something you're interested in introducing to your medicine chest, there's probably no need for you to plant any. Just let your lawn grow for a bit and watch them sprout up as if by magic. If you don't have a lawn, just go to the nearest grassy area in search of cuttings, and odds are you'll have a full harvest before you know it.

As a natural diuretic, dandelion greens are particularly useful because they actually increase the amount of potassium in your system rather than deplete it, as many synthetics do. So these leafy greens, best harvested young for a sweeter flavor, are excellent against water retention and mild kidney problems. There's a good reason, in other words, that dandelion greens are a staple in salads all over the world. The Mediterranean region in particular has a number of recipes that incorporate the health benefits of the greens with the unique flavor of the cooked flowers and the traditional spices of the regions in Italy and Greece where the dish is most popular.

**Dandelions are members of the daisy family, despite their bad reputation.**

SPECIAL SECTION

**TOO EFFECTIVE?** In French, dandelions are *pissenlit*, which means, "wet the bed."

SPECIAL SECTION

**BEING PRICKLY**
This flower's name comes from the Greek word for hedgehog.

# Echinacea

**benefits**

## quick facts

- Those suffering from leukemia should not use echinacea as its effects on the blood are altered in those stricken with the disease.

- Also known as Sampson root, echinacea is deer-resistant, which means it's a valuable herb to place outside of a large outdoor garden to keep the herbivores away.

- While it is a powerful preventative against colds, if one persists for more than two days, it's best to switch to a different treatment specifically suited to your symptoms.

THE KING OF convalescent herbs, echinacea can help purify the blood of toxins while recovering from injury or illness—even a snake bite. It's a natural antiseptic, mild stimulant and diaphoretic (perspiration inducer), so it can attack impurities from all proverbial angles. The roots and leaves of this plant, whose beautiful flowers will also be an aesthetic boon to your garden, can be used to make a powerful tincture or decoction, but can also be applied directly as a poultice on cuts and scrapes to reduce the risk of infection.

Echinacea root may also be able to increase white blood cell production, which means it's ideal to take when folks at the office or in your family are getting sick. Those extra white blood cells will help you fend off disease if you use echinacea for a day or two. It's no surprise, considering these powerful restorative and preventative properties, that echinacea was traditionally given to those who were severely weakened by illness or infection. It was known even in ancient times to stimulate the appetite and improve digestion, which allows the body to take in the nutrients it needs to get back to 100 percent.

**Some herbalists have reported headaches from prolonged echinacea use, so use in moderation.**

# Elder

**benefits**

## quick facts

- Elder can appear either as a large shrub or small tree, growing up to 20 feet with white, star-shaped flowers.

- Elder leaf can be used in a salve that cools burns, and is also valuable in eyewashes and compresses.

- Another herbal cure with some whimsical names in its past (and present), elder is also known as pip tree and devil's wood.

THE MEDICINAL PROPERTIES of the berries, flowers and leaves of this large shrub enjoyed a moment in the spotlight during the H1N1 (Swine Flu) scare of 2009 thanks to research suggesting the long-held traditional belief that elder is a powerful agent against viral illness. Tonics made of elderberries take advantage of the incredible amounts of vitamin C in the plant, as well as the flavonoids, which support everyday cellular maintenance.

Elderberries are also very strong decongestants, but not necessarily just the typical flu-type nasal kind. Elderberry works to remove deeply held congestion from organs like the kidneys and lungs as well as from the joints. A delicious decoction of elder can be made simply by adding 2 teaspoons of elderberries to a cup and a half of water. Simmer it on low while covered and enjoy the taste as it goes to work on your respiratory system first, opening the passageways and dissolving phlegm.

Common, tolerant of aggressive cuts and prunes, and easy to use in medicine, elder has traditionally been thought of as a cure valued among the masses—free, readily available and effective. Berries are produced in fall and can be frozen, preserved, turned into syrup or used in tinctures with a shelf life that should take you through flu season.

**Because the berries of this plant can be buried among dense branches, there is no dedicated equipment for mechanical harvesting.**

SPECIAL SECTION

### elder chaser
If your kids are in the middle of a particularly nasty medicinal regimen—cod liver oil comes to mind—a spoonful of elderberry syrup will knock the aftertaste right out.

# Fennel

**benefits**

## quick facts

- For a natural alternative to pain medication when plagued by cramps, fennel seed has been an herbal standby for centuries.

- In addition to being a great choice for your medicine cabinet, fennel seed introduced into your cooking means a source of vital dietary fiber.

- Due to a high concentration of estrogenic compounds in fennel, women who have or are at high risk for certain types of cancer may want to consult with a doctor before incorporating fennel into any herbal plan.

YOU'LL KNOW IT—and either love or hate it—by its licorice-like taste, but regardless of where you fall in that argument, this humble plant is a tummy ache's worst enemy. Helping to relieve bloating, gas, intestinal pain and other stomach complaints, fennel is safe for kids and adults alike. In fact, the only people who might want to avoid it are pregnant women because fennel has been known to stimulate the uterus as well as the digestive system.

Using fennel for stomach issues, thankfully for those who are anti-licorice, is varied and effective in all its forms. As an essential or herbal oil, for example, fennel can be rubbed onto the abdomen for immediate relief. One teaspoon of fennel seed in a cup of tea steeped for 10 minutes will have a similar effect for an internal approach. A syrup can also be effective, with the added benefit of stimulating and clearing the respiratory system.

Fennel can be found growing freely in many fields, abandoned lots and other open spaces. It is even listed as an invasive species in some areas, so there may be rules against planting it—be sure to check before adding it to your garden. Collect the seeds right after they form, when they're still green.

**Rich in nutrients, fennel can help treat certain cases of anemia.**

SPECIAL SECTION

**WINDBREAKER**
Fennel has been used for generations to alleviate gas.

THE ULTIMATE HOLISTIC HANDBOOK FOR BEGINNERS 115

SPECIAL SECTION

**POWER PACK**
**23%**
of your RDA of Manganese can be found in 1 ounce of garlic.

**Garlic holds myriad health benefits while also being low in calories.**

# Garlic

**benefits**: 🫁 + 👂

## quick facts

- Pickling garlic can reduce the harshness of the raw plant while keeping the medicinal properties intact that might have been lost in cooking.

- To avoid garlic breath, try eating a bit of parsley along with it.

- A garlic clove mixed with 2 tablespoons of olive oil can make an ear oil for the ear infections prone to younger children.

- Garlic is a potent source of germanium, selenium, potassium, magnesium and vitamins C, B and A.

JUST ABOUT the most useful herb you'll find in a naturalist's arsenal, garlic not only tastes great on dishes from around the world, it is also one of the most powerful natural agents against microscopic pests. It's an antiseptic both when used internally and externally, an anti-bacterial so powerful it might even kill antibiotic resistant strains in the right context, and even a vermifuge that can treat intestinal worms and parasites in both humans and their pets.

But despite garlic's appearing ubiquitous and universally safe, it's important to remember a few things. First, garlic can cause indigestion in some, and small children are particularly susceptible to garlic-based acidity. Nursing mothers who notice their children becoming irritated or colicky after feeding should cut garlic out as much as possible. In those with extremely sensitive skin, direct contact with the skin can cause irritation or burns, so gloves might be necessary when working with it.

To grow your own garlic—which allows you to take advantage of the also-edible scape (stalk)—simply save a couple of particularly healthy-looking cloves and plant them point-up, 2 inches deep and half a foot apart. For bigger bulbs, don't prune the scapes as much.

### cold ease

In a trial testing the effects of garlic on cold symptoms, those subjects given a placebo had symptoms for five days. In those given garlic, symptoms lasted only a day and a half.

**THE ULTIMATE HOLISTIC HANDBOOK FOR BEGINNERS**

# Ginger

**benefits**

## quick facts

- Wild ginger, *Asarum canadense*, native to North America is also medicinal but much more powerful, and it can be toxic in large doses. Be sure to stick to Asian ginger.

- Gingerol is the name of the compound that gives ginger its spicy flavor and stimulating properties.

- Ginger plants will go dormant for the cooler winter months. Don't be alarmed if they begin acting strangely with the first cold weather.

MUCH MORE THAN just the garnish next to that spicy tuna roll, ginger root is one of the most commonly used herbal cures in the world. Able to soothe the stomach whether it's upset because of a virus, indigestion or even motion sickness, ginger is second only to garlic in its versatility in the medicine cabinet and the kitchen.

Hot ginger tea with honey is an easy delivery method and can do everything from easing the pain of food poisoning to alleviating menstrual cramps. In addition, it will warm you from the inside and decongest your nose and chest. Similarly, a hot ginger poultice applied directly to the abdomen can relieve all kinds of sharp stomach pain. But the stomach isn't the only body part that can benefit from the ginger treatment. It's long been a cure for pain caused by conditions like arthritis and has even been shown to lower triglyceride levels associated with diabetes.

Extremely popular as an herbal remedy, ginger has no known side effects and can be used safely by all. It's strong enough that chemotherapy patients sometimes use it as an alternative to anti-nausea pharmaceuticals, but mild enough to lend its flavor to candy.

**Ginger before a big meal can help accelerate digestion by half, so you won't feel uncomfortably full.**

SPECIAL SECTION

**ROUGH A.M.?** Ginger is especially effective against morning sickness.

SPECIAL SECTION

**A HOT HERB**
One of ginseng's most common traditional uses was as an aphrodisiac.

# Ginseng

**benefits**

💧 + 🧠 + 🦱

## quick facts

- Ginseng is an all-natural friend to crammers from high school to post-doc. The natural energy boost it can provide doesn't make you crash like coffee or sugar.

- If you find you need a bit of an appetite curber, ginseng has been proven to be a safe way to rein in cravings.

- The name for ginseng's genus, Panax, derives from the Greek words *pan* which means "all" and *akos* which means "cure."

A PERENNIAL KNOWN best in east Asia for its presence in the delicious samgyetang soup, staple of Korean comfort food, ginseng in both its American (*Panax quinquefolius*) and Asian (*Panax ginseng*) iterations are packed with holistic cures.

Ginseng can provide an energy boost, which is why you're likely to find it in the ingredients list of many energy drinks, especially those claiming a natural base. But a bit of a pick-me-up isn't all ginseng can provide when used as a part of a balanced holistic regimen. In a 2014 review and analysis of studies regarding ginseng's effect on type 2 diabetes, the plant was found to be beneficial in regulating hemoglobin levels. However, it may interfere with some kinds of diabetes medications, so be sure to consult with your doctor before adding it to your treatment plan.

Perhaps the most egalitarian use of ginseng is as a powerful antioxidant. Legions of holistic practitioners swear by its ability to reduce the signs of aging. Whether or not ginseng will maintain your youth *Dorian Gray*-style remains to be scientifically proven, but antioxidants themselves are extremely useful in neutralizing free radicals (toxic byproducts of your body's oxygen metabolism). Taking ginseng orally by capsule or in tea or other edibles can protect your body from the degeneration of these free radicals.

**In addition to its other benefits, ginseng may help prevent hair loss if used topically.**

# Goat's Rue

**benefits**

## quick facts

- Because goat's rue is so effective at regulating blood sugar, ingestion should be ceased two weeks before any surgery, as the surgery will likely affect these levels and confuse the treatment.

- The Catawba tribe of Native Americans traditionally used goat's rue as a natural way to reduce fever.

- Goat's rue is common across the eastern U.S. and as far west as Texas, but in New England there are some conservation issues associated with the plant, so check its status in your area if you happen to be a New England herbalist.

ALSO KNOWN AS professor's weed, this all-natural powerhouse has been a boon to expecting and new mothers for centuries. As a known galactagogue—the $10 word for breast-milk enhancer—goat's rue is the best organic way to make sure the family's new addition has enough to eat. One thing new mothers should be aware of is that the herb can interfere with certain diuretic prescriptions, so if you're taking one it's necessary to consult with your doctor before introducing goat's rue to your regimen.

In addition to its postnatal benefits, goat's rue has a history going back to the middle ages in the treatment of type 2 diabetes. In fact, it was a main component in the manufacture of metformin, the current standard in diabetes treatment. This is due to the herb containing an alkaloid that decreases insulin resistance.

Goat's rue can be identified by its hollow stems and hardy leaflets. With long stalks covered in purple-white flowers, the herb can be found more or less wherever livestock is present and is considered a noxious weed in most jurisdictions, so it's better to keep it away from your garden.

---

**Though it can be medicine for humans, most livestock find goat's rue toxic.**

SPECIAL SECTION

**REAL ESTATE HOG**
Goat's rue is an invasive species that can take over entire fields if left unchecked.

## plague plant
Germans called goat's rue *Pestilenzkraut* ("plague herb") because of its reputation for curing infectious diseases, and in England a concoction of goat's rue was used as a specific against the black death.

THE ULTIMATE HOLISTIC HANDBOOK FOR BEGINNERS 123

SPECIAL SECTION

**SWEAT IT OUT**
Goldenrod may help open the pores during a fever.

# Goldenrod

**benefits**

## quick facts

- Goldenrod has a long history of use in Europe for urinary tract infections, and it does appear to be a diuretic with particular use in these situations, though an official scientific study has yet to prove its worth.

- Some folks have traditionally blamed goldenrod for seasonal allergies, but this is a misconception based on the fact that goldenrod and ragweed, which is highly allergenic, bloom at the same time.

- People with blood pressure conditions, whether their pressure is too high or too low, should consult a doctor before introducing goldenrod to an herbal regimen.

THE FLOWER so striking it inspired a Crayola color heralds the valuable leaves and stems underneath. Goldenrod works closely with the lungs and bladder to support the mucus membranes and is a particularly strong help with the residual congestion that often plagues one after a bad cold. The plant will help break it all up and move it all out. This makes it a good choice for allergy sufferers who tend to feel most affected in the lungs.

Goldenrod is also used in traditional cures for bladder incontinence because of its anti-inflammatory and antiseptic properties, which clean and heal the bladder and allow you to find comfort without immediate knowledge of a bathroom in the area. A tonic for chronically infected bladders, goldenrod may also help cure the small holes that can form in the organ as a result of these infections, which leads to painful incontinence.

Goldenrod can also be made into a very effective eye wash for itchy eyes brought on by allergic reactions to pollen or other stimuli. Steep 3 tablespoons of leaves and stems per pint of water for a whole hour. Then douse cotton balls in the infusion and douse each (closed) eye repeatedly. You should find that the herbal remedy has cooled and soothed your itchy and irritated peepers.

**Combines well with plantain, yarrow and St. John's Wort to make a healing salve for the skin.**

## benefits

# Hawthorn

### quick facts

- If you happen to plant hawthorn on your land, you may also want to set up a birdhouse or two—the berries are a favorite of scores of species of birds in both Europe and North America.

- Hawthorn is generally considered safe to use in conjunction with heart medication, but because every case is different, it's best to work with your doctor when bringing hawthorn into your holistic healing plan.

- Hawthorn can refer to a number of closely related species of the genus *Crataegus*. All are considered safe and have been used successfully in natural remedies.

THIS EXTREMELY HARDY PLANT can live to be 200 years old and can grow thickly enough to fence in entire areas of land in the Irish countryside in which it grows most abundantly. But hawthorn can be found in more locales than just the Emerald Isle, and its uses range from tasty syrups made from its berries to astringents and circulation boosters from its constituent parts.

Hawthorn, which is also known in some areas as May blossom or Maybush, finds its primary use in the medicine cabinet as perhaps the most heart-healthy herb that novice holistic practitioners work with. Rich in flavonoids, vitamin B & C, pectin and calcium, the plant works to strengthen the heart muscle through dilating capillaries, which frees blockages and allows blood to flow more freely through the body. It can be used to treat various blood pressure conditions as well as edema, angina, arrhythmia and other heart conditions.

Hawthorn is readily available at nurseries across the country, and once you get yours growing you'll notice that it self-sows regularly, so if you have the space for a beautiful bounty of hawthorn, simply let it go. It is probably for this, as well as its association with the heart, that spiritualists associate hawthorn with bravery, power and the vital life force.

**Also known as thornapple, hawthorn fruit can grow to about the size of a crabapple.**

SPECIAL SECTION

**ROSY OUTLOOK**
Hawthorn is a member of the same family as the rose.

THE ULTIMATE HOLISTIC HANDBOOK FOR BEGINNERS 127

SPECIAL SECTION

**PREVENT**
Chinese studies suggest hops may work to prevent Alzheimer's.

# Hops

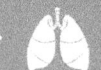

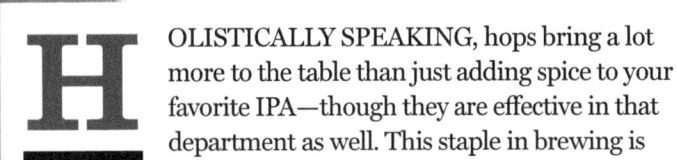

**benefits**

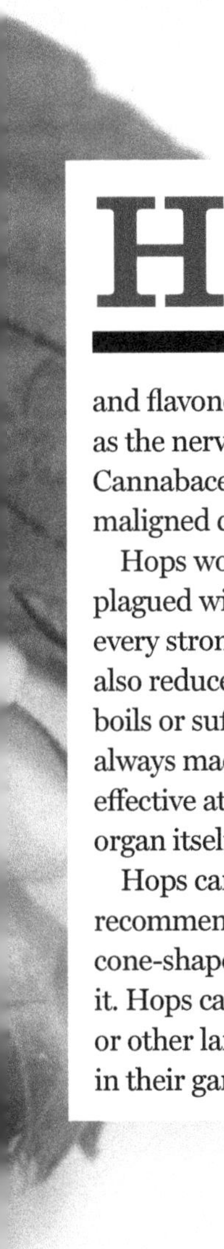

## quick facts

- Hops have been used as a traditional remedy for respiratory complaints, including asthma and dry cough.

- A small contradiction with hops is that though they like to grow tall, they are susceptible to wind, so be sure to anchor them to something sturdy to grow on.

- Herbalists tend to get the best result with seed planted six weeks before the last frost date of the winter in 70-degree soil.

HOLISTICALLY SPEAKING, hops bring a lot more to the table than just adding spice to your favorite IPA—though they are effective in that department as well. This staple in brewing is also rich in natural digestive bitters, vitamin C and flavonoids, which give the digestive system as well as the nerves a relaxing hit. As a member of the family Cannabaceae, hops share some properties with their more maligned cousin, cannabis.

Hops work to calm an overactive central nervous system plagued with anxiety and can help those who tend to feel every strong emotional reaction in their stomach. They can also reduce pain and inflammation, especially in those with boils or suffering from a toothache. For those who haven't always made the best choices in their diet, hops can be effective at normalizing your gastric juices and relaxing the organ itself.

Hops can even be used to treat insomnia. Some herbalists recommend filling a small pillow with hops strobiles (the cone-shaped flowers also used in brewing) and sleeping with it. Hops can be found growing in a climbing fashion up trees or other large, vertical items, so many folks who plant hops in their garden will use a thick stake to encourage the climb.

**Paradoxically, beer hops might be able to increase liver function.**

# Horny Goat Weed

## benefits

## quick facts

- Horny goat weed is also known as Barrenwort and Xian Ling Pi. It is also sometimes referred to by its active ingredient, icariin.

- In some patients, horny goat weed has been known to slow blood clotting, so if this is already a problem for you it's best to consult with a physician, especially before surgery.

- In good news for osteoporosis patients, horny goat weed has been shown to increase bone density.

WHAT'S IN A NAME? Sometimes a great deal, as in the case of horny goat weed, also hilariously known as bishop's hat. First used by ancient goatherds who wanted to increase the population of their flocks, this herb may both increase sex drive (in humans as well as goats) and help treat infertility and impotence. By opening up the blood vessels leading to the brain and the reproductive organs, it supports an increased blood supply to those regions.

For men, horny goat weed has been shown to tone the liver, which may lead to the evening of certain sexual hormones but is valuable in and of itself, as the liver is fundamental in cleansing the body of toxins. Horny goat weed has also been tested in trials regarding erectile dysfunction and has been shown to be able to prevent all aspects of the ailment from start to finish.

The plant can also be used to stimulate kidney and bladder function by toning the bladder and increasing urinary retention while stimulating increased creatinine production in the kidneys.

Horny goat weed can be identified in the wild by its heart-shaped leaves and long flowers and can be used in capsules or infusions.

> **Icariin, the active compound in horny goat weed, has been shown to duplicate the effects of testosterone in rats.**

SPECIAL SECTION

**NEW USE?** Studies are underway to determine if icariin might be a treatment for bipolar disorder.

THE ULTIMATE HOLISTIC HANDBOOK FOR BEGINNERS 131

# Hydrangea

**benefits**

## quick facts

- The greatest variety of species of this flower can be found in east Asia, including Korea, Japan, Northern China and Eastern Russia.

- Taken in large doses, hydrangea can be toxic and is a powerful diuretic, so use sparingly.

- The hydrangea plant can grow to be 9 feet tall.

YOU'LL WANT TO GIVE hydrangea pride of place in your garden once you realize that in addition to being useful in your medicine chest, it's also a bouquet-worthy flower that will add interesting shapes and incredible brightness to your setup. A natural diuretic that also contains calcium, hydrangea can help you overcome most kidney and bladder ailments. It can help with stones and frequent urination as well as clean the urinary tract and dissolve gravel. It has also been shown to relieve prostate swelling.

Because hydrangea works to cleanse the bladder and kidneys, it is also known to clear up certain skin conditions caused by excess water. In conditions like eczema where this is the basis of the complaint, hydrangea can help decongest the skin tissues causing symptoms.

You can recognize hydrangea in the wild by its spherical clumps of small, white, blue or purple flowers. It grows best in full to partial shade.

To make a useful decoction with the roots of this beautiful plant, use a couple of teaspoons per cup, simmering about the length you would for a normal cup of tea. Enjoy up to three cups a day. If you'd prefer to use a tincture to get the direct benefits of hydrangea, use up to 30 drops up to three times a day.

**The root of the hydrangea is sometimes called seven bark herb.**

SPECIAL SECTION

**HOLIDAY TOT**
Add some hydrangea root to your holiday mulled wine or cider for an herbal kick.

SPECIAL SECTION

**TAKE YOUR TIME** It isn't until the second year of growth that juniper berries take on their blue-black color.

# Juniper

**benefits**

## quick facts

- According to spiritualists, juniper's flower essence can help people break free of ancestral patterns and become their own people.

- To make a juniper infusion to ease stomach pain and release toxins from your kidneys and bladder, take up to a teaspoon of crushed berries and combine with a cup of water. Let steep for up to three hours.

- Juniper thrives in dry conditions and does best among pine woods.

THE BERRIES OF this plant are famous for adding a distinctive flavor to your gin and tonics, but they, as well as the bark and the leaves of juniper, have an impact far beyond the bar. In a holistic regimen, this natural diuretic, stimulant and analgesic is one of the easiest and most pleasant-tasting plants to use. Able to stimulate the kidneys and bladder, as well as the mucus membranes, stomach and uterus, juniper has been the subject of medical experimentation for centuries.

Some of the earliest of these experiments resulted in the spirits that would eventually evolve into gin, but the plant itself requires no alchemical aspirations to put to good use. Simply eating a few (up to five) of the berries can soothe an upset stomach, and a juniper infusion can clear your kidneys. Some herbalists even swear by juniper as a brain tonic, which jibes with its use in Chinese traditional medicine as a method of clearing the body of phlegm, thought to be the main cause of brain fog.

Juniper leaves, though, might have the most interesting use of all. Because they contain a natural antibiotic called podophyllotoxin, these scaly leaves may be effective at treating tumors. To avoid any adverse side effects, it's best to discontinue juniper use after six weeks. If you have a history of kidney problems it's best to consult with a doctor before use, as your organs might find it a bit too stimulating for your own good.

**There are as many as 70 different varieties of juniper, many of which are used to create different gins.**

# Lady's Slipper

**benefits**

## quick facts

- Lady's slipper can also be used to promote perspiration, making it a good addition to a fever treatment.

- Because of its similarities to valerian, lady's slipper is sometimes known as American Valerian.

- The Chippewa tribe placed dried and remoistened lady's slipper root directly onto skin inflammations and toothaches as a pain reliever.

CLOSELY RELATED TO *Valeriana officinalis*, which herbalists have used for centuries to relieve stress and promote physical relaxation, lady's slipper shares this use with its cousin but is much milder. Specifically used against frayed nerves rather than tight muscles, lady's slipper can help stress-related insomnia sufferers find their 40 winks. But there's more to this plant than just acting as a less filling, better tasting version of valerian. It can also be a powerful natural pain reliever when obstructions in tissues and muscles are caused by tension. Lady's slipper relaxes the affected area and promotes blood flow, reducing pain.

Lady's slipper is endangered in the wild, so it should never be picked. It will, however, grow long elliptical leaves and the trademark orchid flowers that give the plant its names, from lady's slipper to moccasin plant to Venus shoe. The burnt orange rhizomes are used in medicine and can be made into a decoction by combining a single tablespoon per cup and simmering for 10 minutes, covered.

Lady's slipper was highly prized by Native American tribes across the northeast as a pain reliever for menstrual cramps and labor pains. Because it has no narcotic effects, like valerian, it is safe to use during childbirth, when pregnant and when nursing. Because of its calming qualities, it was also prescribed often during the 19th century obsession with "hysteria," the supposed female-centric disease characterized by extreme stress and emotional demonstration. Hysteria might have been a crock, but the plant's ability to calm users wasn't, and it remains commonly taken to this day.

**Effective as a pain reliever, lady's slipper may help with neuralgia.**

SPECIAL SECTION

**STRONG SCENT**
Lady's slipper has a pungent odor that many find unpleasant.

SPECIAL SECTION

**KINGLY HERB**
Lavender was an essential part of the mummification process in ancient Egypt.

# Lavender

**benefits**

IF LAVENDER ONLY lent its color and scent to your garden, it might nevertheless be one of the most calming plants on hand. The familiar smell and tall, beautiful blooms make lavender the quintessential bridge between an herb garden and a flower garden. But lavender's beauty is only the beginning of its story—in the regions of southern France and the Mediterranean where the plant grows most abundantly, herbalists have known for generations that despite being the belle of the ball, lavender is also a mild antidepressant, a migraine reliever (when used in tandem with feverdew), an antibacterial and dozens of other valuable classifications.

Traditionally, lavender has been an integral part of the birthing process and can be used both as a poultice to give relief and comfort to the mother and as one of the herbs traditionally used in a newborn's first bath, though few herbalists recommend this today. The gentle effects of the plant are also well-suited to being used in the bath as a stress reliever. A few drops of essential oil in the tub will provide natural relief and guarantee one of the most comforting baths of your life.

Lavender can grow pretty large if left in the full sunlight it prefers, so be sure that when planting, you leave enough room that the full-grown plants won't get crowded, between 12" and 24" between plants. Lavender doesn't respond well to overwatering, so make sure to give it a good soaking when necessary and then leave it alone.

## quick facts

- When combined with tea tree oil, lavender is a powerful agent against fungal infections like ringworm.

- Lavender eye pillows are a common remedy for those who have trouble sleeping on planes or trains, as they relieve eye strain and provide a calming scent that helps many nod off.

- To make a lavender massage oil to rub your stress away, simply take an ounce and a half of dried lavender buds and combine with 4 ounces of the nut, vegetable or seed oil of your choice. Finish off with a few drops of lavender essential oil and leave the closed jar in a sunny place for two or three weeks.

**Most lavender flowers are purple, but some varieties can be found in pink or white.**

SPECIAL SECTION

## peas in a pod?
It may seem surprising to those of us who are used to licorice's taste appearing in our sweets, but this plant is actually a member of the pea family.

HOLIDAY
On April 12, the U.S. celebrates national licorice day.

# Licorice

### benefits

### quick facts

- Licorice is a proven adrenal tonic, which means that when you've lost your get-up-and-go due to overworked flight or fight responses, licorice can bounce you back.

- When dealing with herbal teas that aren't exactly number one on the taste scale, adding a small amount of licorice to the brew can often help make the potion more palatable.

- By the same token, a tea made entirely with licorice can often be too strong and sweet for many, so blending a licorice-based cure with other herbs to soften the taste is common as well.

FIFTY TIMES SWEETER than processed table sugar, it's no surprise licorice has been gracing the sweet shops and candy stashes of the world for centuries. But the benefits of licorice don't stop with the nostalgia you get from biting into some: glycyrrhizic acid, which is the compound responsible for the sweet taste of licorice, is a strong anti-inflammatory when broken down in the stomach. Able to effectively relieve arthritis pain through this component, licorice is also responsible for warding off infections such as herpes through phytohormones that are present in the plant and strengthening the endocrine system.

Whether it's due to sore throat, bronchitis, arthritis, bowel irritation or stomach complaints, licorice is one of the world's oldest established remedies for the inflammation that causes much of the relevant discomfort. Singers have often used licorice to bring their voices back up to par after illness—licorice reduces the inflammation caused by overuse and its sweet, syrupy flavor helps coat the throat. Thanks to glycyrrhizic acid, it's also able to relieve both peptic and gastric ulcers. Glycyrrhizic acid, however, has been known to stress the heart and other organs, so those with a history of high blood pressure should consult with a doctor before use.

A mild and gentle laxative, one part licorice can also be used in tandem with one part dandelion root and a half part of yellow dock root. Mix the chopped roots well and make a decoction with up to 2 teaspoons per cup. Drink a cup as needed.

Though traditionally licorice has been thought to act as an estrogen stimulator, this is a common misconception. The plant contains phytohormones rather than actual human hormones and provides only the raw material the liver and endocrine system eventually turn into hormones. So even though licorice does eventually aid in the production of estrogen in women, it also aids in the production of other hormones as well and isn't necessarily a specific for estrogen production.

## benefits

🫁 + 🧑‍🦲 + 😷

# Lungwort

## quick facts

• Though it isn't a nursery staple, lungwort can be found through online retailers including Amazon for those who don't have the room or inclination to grow their own.

• According to flower essence practitioners, lungwort can help those who are caught in the duality between the physical and the metaphysical worlds.

• In vogue as a medical treatment during the crusades, lungwort is also known as Jerusalem sage and Bethlehem sage.

FOUND GROWING on the bark of trees such as oak, beech or maple, or even on rocks, lungwort gets its name because the leaf-like growth is covered in nooks and crannies that resemble the structure of a human lung. Because of this resemblance, ancient herbalists associated it with the respiratory system through the doctrine of signatures, which stated that the best uses for herbs and plants were indicated by their appearance. Because it takes up to 30 years to grow, it isn't commonly available in nurseries, but those who can find lungwort will be introducing a useful anti-swelling agent that helps both respiratory complaints and sinusitis.

"The Lung Cleansing Benefits of Lungwort," a study published by the Global Healing Center, claims that other studies had proved that lungwort has a higher concentration of antioxidants than any of the 20 species tested, meaning that in addition to its anti-swelling properties it can also be incredibly healthful in preventing signs of aging.

Though the leaf-like growths are notoriously jagged-looking, Lungwort produces flowers that make it a staple in English gardens (Lungwort prefers darker, damper climes) as well as in herbal medicine chests. So not only will your garden be gaining a plant capable in clinical trial of curing 82 percent of sinusitis complaints within a week, but it will also gain some wonderful color and an interestingly shaped, intriguingly pretty plant.

**Though it appears leaf-like, lungwort is actually a member of the kingdom fungi.**

SPECIAL SECTION

## pulmonaria
Not to be confused with the lungwort parasite, lungwort is also a nickname for the flower pulmonaria, native to Europe and central Asia. The flower blooms early in spring, before many have even budded.

SPECIAL SECTION

**ENDANGERED**
More than 20 species of mistletoe are at risk.

# Mistletoe

**benefits**

THE PLANT BEST known for making hearts flutter—or nerves fray—at Christmas parties is actually one of nature's best-proven ways to lower high blood pressure and improve general circulation. Those with an irregular heartbeat and some cardiac obstructive diseases may also find that mistletoe tincture under the tongue can return heartbeat and breath to normal, allowing for rest.

Mistletoe's proven ability to improve circulation is also extremely helpful for those who suffer from delirium, convulsion or seizures by opening up the body's passages and preventing blockages. Muscle spasms and pain can be caused by similar circulation issues, and mistletoe's ability to smooth muscle tissue by improving blood flow can help with these as well.

Though pregnant women shouldn't use mistletoe in their herbal regimen because it can cause uterine contractions, this side effect has been successfully used to induce labor at the right time for generations in traditional cultures. In fact, pelvic congestion in general, both uterine and prostate-related, can be relieved by mistletoe, once again because it aids in delivering fluids to the parts of the body that need them most.

## quick facts

- Some herbalists are convinced of mistletoe's ability to help eliminate cancer cells, but these claims have yet to be supported by adequate research.

- Mistletoe's nickname, "all heal," speaks to its traditional importance in many cultures—in Europe, it is still so popular as a cure that it is available as an injection and as supplements, and it is readily available.

- Mistletoe is technically a parasitic shrub that lives by attaching itself to other plants and prefers deciduous trees with malleable bark.

**Mistletoe can be toxic if eaten raw or taken in some preparations, so consult with an expert before exploring its medical properties.**

**benefits**

# Mullein

## quick facts

- Once you learn what mullein is, you may find yourself noticing it wherever you go. It takes to dense woods as well as open prairie, yards in suburbia and anywhere else you can think of. You might even drive past some next time you're on a highway with a particularly grassy divider.

- Some people with sensitive skin might find that mullein flowers directly applied to the skin can cause irritation, but if a remedy calls for doing so, wrapping the flowers in cheesecloth before use is generally effective.

MULLEIN'S HISTORY as a healing herb is so long and storied that among its first uses was the banishment of supposed evil spirits causing illness. Regardless of whether the lung complaints most often treated with the beautiful, yellow-flowered plants were actually the work of imps or demons, the shamanic healers who first put the stuff to use were on to something. Useful for bringing water to places in the body that need it, such as the upper respiratory tract during a dry coughing spell, mullein helps the lungs' cilia function normally.

Also known as blanket herb and old lady's flannel because of the familiar look and feel of its flowers, mullein is a well-known analgesic, antibacterial, astringent, expectorant, mild sedative, antispasmodic and emollient. What this mouthful means for you is that the flowers and leaves of this plant can not only help you breathe easy after a cough, it can also calm your irritated nerves, lubricate your joints, relieve mucus congestion, ease spasms and even treat asthma. Traditional Native American remedies for this latter condition even had sufferers smoke mullein along with other healing herbs, though this treatment has fallen out of fashion.

Technically a weed, like the equally useful dandelion, mullein appears more like an exotic flower, with its stout leaf bases giving way to towering stalks of yellow flowers that can reach a few feet in the air. These flowers, when turned into an oil-based cure, can naturally relieve the pain of an ear infection while cleaning the ear in the process.

**A 2001 study found ear drops containing mullein were just as effective as anesthetic ones in treating an ear infection.**

SPECIAL SECTION

**MULLEIN PUFF**
In some Native American traditions, mullein is a key component in smoked remedies.

THE ULTIMATE HOLISTIC HANDBOOK FOR BEGINNERS 147

SPECIAL SECTION

**STING SO GOOD?** Strangely, nettle can be crafted into a pain-relieving topical ointment.

# Nettle

**benefits**

## quick facts

● Nettle helps the body process protein and move waste aspects of protein, which makes it a great supplement for those fitness-oriented folks who are trying to build muscle, as well as anyone enjoying a "paleo" diet.

● Nettles are considered a safe medicine for people of all ages, as long as gloves are worn when it's picked.

● Some people may find that nettle can cause dry mouth and constipation, but these symptoms can be counteracted by combining nettle with a more elementally moist herb.

THE MOST FAMOUS ancient use of nettle was devised by the Romans, who treated arthritis and bursitis pain by tying stalks of nettle together and flogging the affected regions in a process called urtication. While this may seem like a remedy that has been rightly lost to time, the strange part about it is that urtication is still a widely used and trusted natural remedy for those same conditions, and those who use it claim it provides relief without the myriad side effects with which many pain relief prescriptions can saddle users. This is probably why the Greeks and Romans cultivated more nettles in their lands than any other crop.

Apart from its well-known sting, nettle is one of the most bountiful plants in nature when it comes to making patients feel good. Useful for everything from relieving growing pains in young children to doing the same for the creaky joints of old age, nettles grow wild throughout the U.S. and Canada. You can create a tincture from the leaves to take orally, but a lot of people also enjoy simply steaming up a pot of nettle greens for pain relief benefits. A common component in premenstrual syndrome formulas and prostate tonics, nettles are also beneficial to the reproductive health of both men and women.

To create a nettle green tea that will act as a tonic for tired and painful bones as well as help your body fend off illness and relieve hay fever, steep the dried herb for up to 10 minutes. But when planting nettles it's important to place them where you won't easily brush up against them and receive a "sting," which can leave painful welts.

**Once cooked, nettles no longer sting and can be added to soups and stews for a healthy bite.**

# Oats

## benefits

## quick facts

- To harvest oats from the plant, simply hold a receptacle like a bucket or basket under the plant and gently run your fingers up through the pats, letting them gently detach and fall into the container.

- In combination with lemon balm, oat "milk" can also be used as a cure for hyperactivity in children and adults.

- Before planting seeds for your own oats, be sure to soak the seeds overnight and sow directly into the soil in the morning.

IN ADDITION to being one of the first grains planted by humans during the neolithic revolution, oats are also one of the most nutritious and culturally long-lived in the world. Both the milky flower tops and the stalks, known as oatstraw, are beneficial for animals as well as humans and contain vitamins E, B and D. Oats are also rich in natural proteins and alkaloids, and their "milk" is a well-known nervine, meaning it can be used for an all-natural soothing of your nerves.

But today's herbalists and health-conscious eaters will undoubtedly know oats for their heart-healthy and delicious breakfast derivative, oatmeal. Made from fully ripe oats, oatmeal has enjoyed FDA heart-healthy status since 1998 and has been shown to both decrease levels of "bad" cholesterol and increase levels of "good" cholesterol.

Once the oats have been harvested, however, the most powerful medicinal part of the plant still remains. The oatstraw contains silica for strong bones, teeth, nails and hair. It also has been shown to be one of the best natural remedies for the nervous system, eliminating stress, irritation and anxiety. For this use, oatstraw baths have been a common prescription for generations—simply use 4 tablespoons of oatstraw per quart of bathwater and steep for two hours. Strain and soak.

**Oats are a gluten-free whole grain, making them a healthy choice for those cutting down on gluten.**

## a pox on you?

Oatmeal baths are a tried and true method for alleviating the discomfort that comes with chicken pox. A warm bath blended with two cups of ground oatmeal can soothe the painful condition.

THE ULTIMATE HOLISTIC HANDBOOK FOR BEGINNERS 151

# Oregon Grape

**benefits**

## quick facts

- Though the fruits of Oregon grape look like tasty dark berries, it's actually the root and rhizome that are used medicinally.

- For an Oregon grape decoction, take up to 2 teaspoons of root per cup and steep for 12 minutes with a cover.

- Those herbalists who believe in flower essence therapy use Oregon grape to relieve paranoid or defensive behavior.

SPANISH SETTLERS in the New World called Oregon grape the herb of the blood, and its healing properties are still renowned today with regard to circulation. Oregon grape, also known as rocky mountain grape or California barberry, works with the liver to release iron into the bloodstream, which increases hemoglobin levels and ensures extremely low toxicity levels in the blood. Because it's so good at working with the liver, however, if you're taking any liver medications, Oregon grape may interfere with them, so it's best to consult a physician before use.

In addition to the blood benefits that were honed in the era of the conquistadors, Oregon grape is also one of your digestive system's best friends. It can increase appetite in those who are convalescing, improve digestion and assimilation, and even regulate your metabolism. And if that food happens to present its own problems, Oregon grape is the herbalist's proven cure for rapid-onset diarrhea.

Oregon grape is also extremely good at stimulating the growth of new cells in the body, which makes it valuable as a skin-care aid. Replacing dead skin cells with shiny new ones is the easiest and most effective way of making your skin appear younger, and Oregon grape is a powerhouse for that process.

**Herbalists who have grown used to the now-endangered goldenseal will find a ready replacement here.**

SPECIAL SECTION

**Seven**
maximum number of days an adult should use Oregon grape consecutively

THE ULTIMATE HOLISTIC HANDBOOK FOR BEGINNERS

# Pennyroyal

**benefits**

## quick facts

- Pennyroyal is a member of the mint family native to the Eurasian land mass as well as Britain and Ireland. Its American equivalent can be found all over North America.

- After the last frost of the year, it's safe to sow your pennyroyal directly into the ground.

- Pennyroyal was first mentioned in Greek literature as early as 421 B.C. in the plays of Aristophanes.

DENSELY PACKED WITH violet flowers that will add a pleasing color to any garden, pennyroyal is among the most time-tested Native American cures for stomach complaints, especially those accompanied by a fever. Whether it's a simple upset stomach or a complaint more similar to heartburn or indigestion, pennyroyal can ease pain with its cooling nature as well as instigate perspiration to help break a fever. So next time you're plagued by a 24-hour bug, it might be wise to reach for some pennyroyal before you go for the prescription meds.

However, a far more common use of pennyroyal in traditional circles was to bring about delayed menses when one's cycle was interrupted by stress, sickness, suppression or other concerns. Or if your period comes with extreme pain or drastic uterine spasms, pennyroyal can help by thinning the uterine walls and easing the process. Pennyroyal can sometimes induce miscarriage because of this ability, but this has not, as far as is known, ever been a widespread traditional function, and pennyroyal is not considered a safe abortifacient.

Another caution to take when working with pennyroyal is to be keenly aware of the fact that pennyroyal essential oil can be toxic if taken orally or used topically. Infusions and tinctures are the safest way to ingest pennyroyal.

**Pennyroyal has been noted to smell like mint leaf when crushed.**

SPECIAL SECTION

**GET CORDIAL**
Fever chills can often be alleviated by a tot of pennyroyal cordial.

THE ULTIMATE HOLISTIC HANDBOOK FOR BEGINNERS 155

SPECIAL SECTION

**POTASSIUM-RICH**
Just 100g of peppermint contains more than 500mg of potassium.

# Peppermint

**benefits**

## quick facts

- Peppermint is a hybrid of watermint and spearmint.

- Peppermint oil contains more than 40 percent menthol, which gives it the cooling, calming scent that herbalists and candymakers prize.

- A study conducted by the University of Adelaide in Australia found that peppermint activates a pain-dulling channel in the colon, meaning inflammatory pains in the abdomen can be reduced through its use.

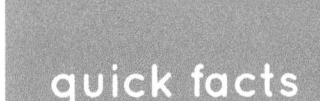

PERHAPS THE MOST familiar and trusted herbal remedy in this collection, peppermint's medical benefits might be topped by the "spoonful of sugar" effect it can often lend to other, fouler-tasting herbal remedies. Adding some peppermint to even the most challenging herbal tea can give it a familiar enough taste to get the medicine down with relative ease. In addition to its taste-bud benefits, peppermint is also among the safest, most effective, beloved, versatile, available plants possible to grow—with ease, to boot.

Among the most common digestive aids in the world, peppermint can be taken after a big meal in the form of tea or, more commonly, as candy, to ensure problem-free digestion. Some chefs even like to add a bit to their pesto for a bit of nutritional value, a kick of flavor and to balance the acidity of the other ingredients.

Less well known than the fact that peppermint is delicious and soothing is the plant's natural ability to relieve pain from headaches and certain burns as well as indigestion and the painful aches that can accompany it. Peppermint tea is a powerful boon when a headache needs to be shortened, and a poultice of peppermint and honey can keep a burn clean while peppermint cools the sting.

**Those with gastroesophageal reflux disease (GRD) should avoid large doses of peppermint.**

SPECIAL SECTION

**SHAKESPEARIAN**
No less an authority than the Bard authorized plantain for broken shins.

# Plantain

**benefits**

## quick facts

- For an all-natural mouthwash that will relieve irritated gums, steep 3 tablespoons of plantain root powder in water for two hours and rinse three times a day.

- If you are taking medication to thin your blood, it is best to avoid large doses of plantain.

- Plantain will grow in any soil and makes a great starter plant for those with enough space to accommodate it. Just don't be surprised when some folks are under the impression your garden is overrun by weeds.

AS A TRADITIONAL remedy for blood poisoning, the leaves, root and stem of the plantain have been used for generations. Considered a weed, much like the dandelion, plantain is among the hardiest and most useful plants that can be added to your garden. Not to be confused with the banana-like fruit used in many delicious dishes, herbal plantain is more of a boon to the skin than the stomach. (Though, the fruit is valuable as well. In 8 ounces of cooked, mashed plantains, health food fanatics can find more than 25 percent of their daily potassium and more than 35 percent each of vitamins A and C.)

Herbal plantain is also one of the finest herbs for poultice-making, and mashed, chopped or chewed leaves can be placed directly onto the problem area. They may even change color, becoming darker, and eventually black, as toxins are drawn from your body. Such a poultice can be used for bites, stings, boils, skin disorders and infections. Plantain tea can even draw out foreign objects too deeply embedded to be pulled out. Simply soak the wound for 20–30 minutes.

Plantain is, in short, a superfood that doesn't always get its due. Because it grows so readily in abandoned lots, backyards and open fields, it hasn't quite made it to the same sort of upper-crust restaurants and treatment plans that, say, avocado has. But in terms of packing a medicinal punch into a tasty and easily available package, it's the stuff of holistic daydreams.

**In the U.S., herbal plantain is sometimes known as snakeweed due to traditional belief in its use as a snake bite cure.**

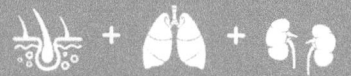

# Poplar

## benefits

## quick facts

- The poplar contains a large amount of salicin, which acts as an anti-inflammatory in the body.

- Poplar is thought to help reduce uric acid, making it a helpful aid for anyone looking to avoid kidney stones.

- Poplar bark and buds used for medicinal purposes should be kept in airtight containers out of the sun.

FEW SIGHTS can stir a love of nature in the observer like a line of poplar trees in full bloom swaying in the wind. But this miraculous plant holds secrets that extend beyond mere beauty.

The dried, unopened leaf buds of the poplar have long been used to help treat a variety of ailments, from minor skin irritations to coughs to hemorrhoids. Found in the temperate regions of the Northern Hemisphere, including the eastern United States and northern Africa, the poplar has been a boon to ancient botanists and modern medicine men alike. "The ointment called Populneon, which is made of this poplar, is singularly good for all heat and inflammations in any part of the body, and tempers the heat of the wounds," wrote 17th century English botanist Nicholas Culpeper in his Complete Herbal and English Physician, penned in 1653.

Today, many advocates of natural healing turn to poplar when troubled by a cough, and the plant is a common ingredient in many herbal cough remedies. When prepared as a balm, poplar can also be applied to skin suffering from sunburn, frostbite or even more sensitive areas afflicted with hemorrhoids, which provides relief, according to the plant's advocates.

Anyone wanting to cultivate their own poplars should find a cutting from a healthy tree and place it in soil made of half peat and half sand. Keep it out of direct sunlight, and make sure the poplar gets plenty of water. Also, the poplar should take root in a part of your garden free from weeds, which tend to overtake young poplars.

**Poplar is also the source of Balm of Gilead, a resinous substance used in perfume-making.**

SPECIAL SECTION

> **SOOTHER**
> In addition to working for respiratory issues, poplar can soothe sore throats.

THE ULTIMATE HOLISTIC HANDBOOK FOR BEGINNERS **161**

## benefits

# Queen of the Me[adow]

### quick facts

- Queen of the Meadow can cause lung spasms, so those with asthma should avoid use.

- Because this plant is similar in its effects to aspirin, taking it in addition to an aspirin regimen or while taking aspirin for pain can cause the side effects of aspirin to magnify.

- Queen of the Meadow's traditional uses in the ancient world included being a cure-all for Celtic druids.

IT MIGHT BE called Queen of the Meadow, but the locker room is where this royal herb proves its worth. For tired, inflamed ligaments and tendons and connective tissues of all kinds, this plant's medicinal remedies can counteract the effects of overwork and poor diet. It can also help strengthen previously injured connective tissue. Rich in salicylic acids that aid in decreasing inflammation, Queen of the Meadow is a key recovery herb for those herbalists who are also of an athletic constitution. These same acids help relieve fever, which is one of Queen of the Meadow's traditional uses.

Another time-tested use of Queen of the Meadow was to cleanse the body of toxic build-ups like those caused by gout. When uric acid accumulates in the small joints, the plant provides pain relief as well as the natural clearance, through urination, of the acid buildup. On the other hand, when diarrhea causes evacuation to be too frequent, Queen of the Meadow's astringent properties mean it can provide relief just as well.

When Queen of the Meadow, also known as meadowsweet, enjoyed a vogue in England during the reign of Queen Elizabeth I, the monarch is supposed to have festooned her chambers with the flowers, then—as now—prized just as much for their appearance and scent as for their healing properties. Rich in calcium, silica and vitamin C, meadowsweet helps the body do its own version of the classic "out with the old, in with the new" routine.

**Queen of the Meadow has seen some nominal success as an aid for those with kidney problems.**

SPECIAL SECTION

**CHEERS!**
Queen of the Meadow is a favorite herb of home-brewers.

THE ULTIMATE HOLISTIC HANDBOOK FOR BEGINNERS  **163**

# Raspberry

**benefits**

## quick facts

- In addition to being delicious, red raspberries are rich in vitamin C and dietary fiber.

- Raspberry leaf tea is an ancient cure for canker sores, cold sores, gingivitis and other oral complaints.

- Before planting, you may find better overall results if you prepare the soil for a couple weeks by beginning to fertilize.

IT'S NO SECRET that the berries of this plant can make a tasty addition to most breakfasts or desserts, but for herbalists, it's the leaves that pack the biggest punch. A time-tested herb used for generations in childbirth, the raspberry plant's leaf can prepare the uterus for delivery as well as help it return to its original size afterward. In addition, it has been known to increase the nutrient content of breast milk, which nicely rounds out raspberry's position in your medicine chest as the master of midwifery.

The leaves of the raspberry plant can also be used to help heal the stomach and intestinal lining. If you are plagued by ulcers, raspberry can help to revitalize and regenerate the stomach tissue and tone the intestinal walls, offering relief from painful conditions like inflammatory pockets, Crohn's disease or IBS.

In the wild, if no berries are present on the plant, raspberry can look almost identical to blackberry. You can tell the difference by noting the prickles (blackberry has fewer, larger thorns and raspberry has more, smaller ones) or the size of the brambles overall. Blackberry bushes tend to be smaller, at an average of five feet. To make raspberry leaf into an infusion, steep 2 tablespoons for 10–12 minutes.

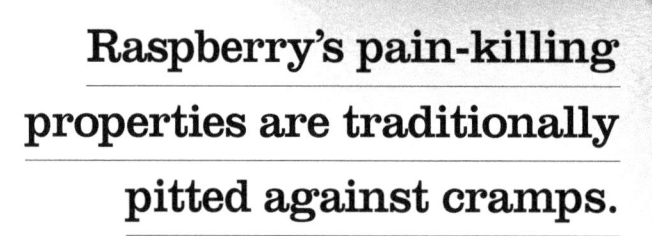

## Raspberry's pain-killing properties are traditionally pitted against cramps.

SPECIAL SECTION

**MEN'S TONIC**
In addition to its benefits for women, raspberry leaf can also help normalize hormone levels in men.

THE ULTIMATE HOLISTIC HANDBOOK FOR BEGINNERS

SPECIAL SECTION

**ROYAL FUNGUS** Reishi has earned the nickname "queen healer" in some herbal circles.

# Reishi

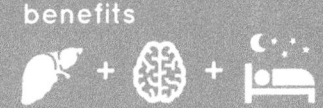

**benefits**

## quick facts

- *Bioorganic & Medicinal Chemistry* published a study in 2009 that showed the polysaccharides found in the reishi mushroom can help to improve longevity.

- A 2013 study published in *Food and Chemical Toxicology* showed that reishi had reversed chemical-driven liver damage in lab mice, opening the door for future testing.

- Because mushrooms compete with mold and bacteria in the wild, as preventatives against these elements in medicine, some mushrooms like reishi are very effective.

FOUND GROWING on hardwoods like oak, elm and maple, reishi is a fan-shaped mushroom that makes its home most often on stumps or fallen logs. But this fungus's lowly origin belies an extremely powerful aid for your central nervous system. By controlling your bodily functions of reaction and relaxation, reishi helps your nervous system know when to act and when to chill. This in turn makes immune reactions more effective.

During a potent cold season when you feel yourself catching every bug you're introduced to, reishi is particularly useful. When the immune system is working overtime, the mushroom can strengthen the parasympathetic nervous system and the adrenal glands to give your immune system a boost. For example, when stress weakens your immune responses, reishi regulates the antibody responses in your system and allows you to fight or prevent infection more effectively. In breast cancer patients, reishi has been shown to alleviate anxiety and depression.

In Chinese and Japanese herbal medicine, reishi also has a place as a cure for insomnia. Reishi's sleep-promoting properties are widely touted in Asian sources, and this use is beginning to catch on in the west as well.

**Reishi is commonly known as Ling Zhi by its myriad advocates in Chinese Traditional Medicine.**

SPECIAL SECTION

**METAL MASTER**
A tablespoon of rosemary contains 45 percent of your daily iron.

# Rosemary

**benefits**

## quick facts

• Rosemary oil is a traditional remedy for thinning hair. The oil is supposed to stimulate the hair follicles.

• One of rosemary's earliest documented purposes was as a memory booster, according to "The Psychopharmacology of European Herbs with Cognition-Enhancing Properties," published in *Current Pharmaceutical Design*, December 2006.

• Rosemary is widely used in aromatherapy to mitigate mood changes.

ROSEMARY'S PRIMARY use for herbalists has dealt with the circulatory system for centuries. Though you might be more used to it on your roasted potatoes, it's within the shaman's arsenal rather than the chef's where the plant's true heritage lies. Promoting flow in your circulatory system, rosemary is so effective it's used as a specific against cardiac edema. It releases buildup in the capillaries and flushes out toxins while stimulating nerves and blood vessels as it moves through the system.

Rosemary has also been used in traditional cures for blood sugar imbalances in the body. By facilitating the breakdown of sugar, it increases the amount of sugar that can be processed, helping prevent symptoms of dysglycemia like dizziness and fatigue.

Rosemary is notoriously difficult to grow from seed, so odds are you'll want to work with cuttings when introducing rosemary to your garden. They are identifiable by their wooden stems, which are covered in needles. These slim, numerous leaves give off a pungent odor that will help identify the plant in the future. Small white and purple flowers can be identified as rosemary by their protruding stamens.

**In medieval Europe, rosemary was believed to thrive only in the gardens of righteous people.**

## benefits

brain + digestion + intestines

# Sage

### quick facts

- Sage is an astringent that can help with gastrointestinal complaints like bloating and flatulence as well as bring appetite back to those who have lost it.

- Along with oregano, lavender, rosemary, thyme and basil, sage is part of the mint family.

- Recent studies have suggested that sage might live up to its adjective synonym in that it can fend off memory loss. Some suggest it may even be key in Alzheimer's research.

IT'S BEEN burned to cast away bad vibes for centuries—ever since those vibes were referred to as demons and a priest rather than a new homeowner would perform the ceremony—but sage is just as useful now as it was to the ancients. Your own supply is likely gathering dust alongside the other spices you only bring out for Thanksgiving stuffing, but a bit of fresh sage in the garden or medicine chest can make all the difference in natural remedies of a surprising number. Also numerous are the sheer number of species in sage's family. There are more than 750 thriving all over the world, and many of them are used in cures both traditional and modern, but most American herbalists will be most familiar with *Salvia officinalis*, which is what we'll cover here.

Sage's most popular use today is as a digestive aid: The herb can help digest rich meals that are high in fat, and its position on the spice rack means that it's most often cooked. However, in Chinese Traditional Medicine, sage is most closely related to the tendons. Increasing blood flow to affected areas, sage can help rejuvenate those tendons that have become dry or sinewy through neglect or overuse. Athletes, for this reason, may find sage useful.

Sage has also been used successfully as a mild sedative especially helpful to those who tend to overthink things. In states such as over-excitement, nervousness and anxiety, especially when accompanied by tremors, sage can promote a calm change. It is, however, only recommended for short-term use and should be avoided by pregnant women thanks to its ability to decrease the flow of breastmilk. Once breastfeeding women are ready to wean, however, sage is extremely useful for the same reason.

**Working wonders on the digestive system, sage helps fight gas.**

SPECIAL SECTION

**FOR PHARAOHS**
In ancient Egypt, sage tea was a remedy used by royalty.

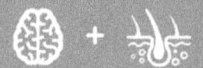

# St. John's Wort

**benefits**

## quick facts

- St. John's Wort oil is an excellent cure for skin ailments like burns, sprains, bruises and other injuries.

- Because of some adverse effects reported when combined with prescription drugs, consult with your health practitioner before adding St. John's Wort to your regimen.

- Traditionally, St. John's Wort has been a key component in treating stubborn skin wounds like bedsores. Because these are essentially pockets of sepsis, the antibacterial and antiviral agents in the plant are effective.

WHEN ASSESSING the effectiveness of herbal cures throughout history, the highest praise one can find is when ancient cultures are so astounded by a plant they simply refer to it as magic. This is the case for St. John's Wort with the ancient Greeks, who felt that the plant was so useful it couldn't entirely be a product of the natural world. Dioscorides, the famous ancient herbalist, used it for his sciatica. Galen included it in his well-known pharmacopoeia. The popularity of St. John's Wort hasn't changed at all over the millennia, though the name of the plant has.

In modern times, one of the most widespread uses of St. John's Wort is to naturally treat depression and seasonal affective disorder. Taken over a two- or three-week period and cycled through a longer time frame if necessary, St. John's Wort has been known to help those who suffer, but many patients have misunderstood the effectiveness of St. John's Wort and expected a drug-like, instantaneous reaction. For effective use, simply supplement your normal regimen with St. John's Wort and expect results after weeks, not minutes.

Because St. John's Wort is also used as an anti-bacterial, anti-inflammatory and antiviral agent, it may be effective against complaints such as herpes. It is so useful, in fact, that the plant has been introduced successfully to herb gardens all over the world and is likely to thrive in yours as well with full sunlight.

---

**In 2009, a study showed that St. John's Wort was more effective than placebos at treating depression.**

SPECIAL SECTION

### the natural way
Because St. John's Wort products like tea have natural antidepressant properties, the herb should not be mixed with prescriptions for depression and can affect other medications including the birth control pill.

## benefits

### quick facts

- Traditionally, thyme has been used as a remedy for bedwetting.

- The Medical and Sanitary Microbiology Department at Medical University of Lodz in Poland recently conducted a study that showed thyme was successful at combating some antibiotic-resistant strains of bacteria.

- Unlike its more common tablemate, salt, thyme actually helps lower blood pressure.

# Thyme

THYME HAS a long enough use in old-fashioned American cures that one of the maladies still listed by many sources as being curable with thyme's help is "whooping cough." Like many of its herbal counterparts, thyme's use in the medicine chest has also been overshadowed by its ability to bring lovely flavors out of chicken, but astute herbalists know that this "spice" is more useful to the healer than the cook. Used in antifungal remedies for generations, thyme was also proven by Dr. Paul Lee of University of California, Santa Cruz to be a specific for the thymus gland, the pristine function of which allows for optimum immune function.

The respiratory tract and throat are also particularly affected by thyme, and it has been a component in vocal remedies for singers and orators for centuries thanks to its soothing feeling and antiseptic effect. It can be turned into a cough syrup thanks to this boon, and a simple rinse with thyme-based mouthwash can kill germs that lead to disease and bad breath.

A thyme salve is particularly useful as a stimulant for the thymus gland and can be rubbed into the upper chest. But thyme honey is also a tasty alternative that will offer mild stimulation as well as the calming effects of thyme. When used in a wash, this completely safe herb can gently fight infection in small wounds.

**In the Middle Ages, thyme was placed in pillows to ward off nightmares.**

SPECIAL SECTION

**HERBAL COURAGE**
Ancient Greeks believed that thyme was a source of bravery.

THE ULTIMATE HOLISTIC HANDBOOK FOR BEGINNERS 175

# Valerian

**benefits**: brain + sleep

## quick facts

- Because valerian works on your body like a sedative, use the same precautions you would with any similar drug regarding driving, operating heavy machinery, etc.

- While the Food and Drug Administration hasn't weighed in on valerian's effectiveness as a sedative, Germany's Commission E (which provides expert, scientific advice to the government regarding substances used in nontraditional remedies) rates valerian as mildly effective.

- Some studies suggest that a person needs to take valerian for a few weeks before it starts working in the body.

THIS COMMON PLANT of European origin delights the eye with its fluffy flowers of white and pink hue, but it's the roots of the valerian plant that make it so sought-after by herbalists. Containing a fluid that emits a sharp, somewhat unpleasant smell, the root of the plant contains a compound still not completely understood by science that may help many find that elusive good night's sleep.

Valerian's potential effect on the human body's nervous system has been experimented on since at least the second century A.D., when the famed Greek physician Galen used it to treat insomnia. Today's advocates of the root follow in Galen's footsteps, turning to valerian when they can't stop tossing and turning in bed. Studies have shown that people taking valerian fell asleep faster and enjoyed a better night's rest than those taking a placebo, without any of the grogginess associated with mainstream medicine's sleeping pills. The exact mechanism through which valerian helps usher us into dreamland isn't understood, but some researchers believe the plant increases the amount of the chemical gamma aminobutyric acid (GABA) in the brain, similar to how the drugs Valium and Xanax work.

Those curious about valerian have a variety of options when it comes to ingesting the drug. Some drink a tea made with dried valerian root an hour or two before bedtime, while others take capsules of a dried powder extract three times a day. Valerian is also available as a tincture and a fluid extract, for those so inclined.

**The first noted use of valerian in medicine was more than 2,000 years ago by the Greek physician Dioscorides.**

SPECIAL SECTION

## root nip
Valerian root is a well-known stimulant for cats who need to get up and get a bit of exercise. This is due to the presence of a compound called actinidine in valerian.

SPECIAL SECTION

**NOT FOR BABY**
Pregnant women and nursing mothers should avoid wild yam.

# Wild Yam

**benefits**

## quick facts

- Certain preliminary studies suggest wild yam may help as an anti-invasive agent for breast cancer, though more research is needed.

- Some Native Americans used wild yam to treat colic or abdominal pain.

- One of the ways wild yam is different than sweet potato yams is that, unlike sweet potato yams, wild yams do not have a fleshy root.

PUT THE FORK AWAY—the yams we're going to be covering have nothing to do with what appears on your Thanksgiving table. But according to many herbalists, wild yam is a plant you should still look forward to ingesting as it can help you through the worst symptoms of a variety of ailments. *Dioscorea villosa*, found natively in both North America and China, has been used for centuries to treat inflammation and asthma. But perhaps even more fascinating, science has confirmed that wild yam roots contain diosgenin, a plant-based hormone similar to the estrogen found in humans.

While scientific studies have yet to confirm any results, many advocates of wild yam claim it can help alleviate menstrual cramps and hot flashes (for women going through menopause). Because certain studies have shown wild yam contains anti-fungal properties, it is also used by some to combat yeast infections. Wild yam is usually ingested in a dry, powdered form (as a capsule) or applied as a topical cream. Because science has yet to confirm wild yam's complete effects on the body, the mainstream medical community recommends that anyone who would ordinarily be wary of ingesting hormones (such as those with a family history of hormone-related cancers, including breast cancer) should avoid wild yam. This also includes women on birth control.

**There are two species of wild yam, one common to North America and the other common to China.**

SPECIAL SECTION

**COLONIST**
Though it is native to North America, Yarrow was also brought to the colonies as part of Europeans' first-aid kits.

# Yarrow

**benefits**

## quick facts

- Infusing yarrow into hair care products may help stimulate follicle growth.

- High heat will destroy yarrow's flavor and makes finished remedies extremely bitter. If cooking with yarrow, add it only at the end of cooking to avoid overheating.

- Yarrow plants should be divided every three to five years.

For any Latin language buffs who also happen to be herbalists, the scientific name of this herbal standby, *Achillea millefolium*, contains a hint as to its appearance. *Millefolium* can be translated as "thousand-leaved," and the petite white flowers conglomerated into ample bundles atop thickly leaved stalks quickly show why. In your garden, yarrow will be one of the most aesthetically pleasing additions, but in the medicine chest it will be even more of a boon.

As what is known as an amphoteric, yarrow moves within the body in the direction it is most needed. It can, for example, perform seemingly contradictory purposes in regulating menstrual flow. Yarrow can stimulate a delayed or absent period and can reduce cramps. However, it can also stop bleeding during a dangerously heavy period. Often mixed with the herb shepherd's purse, yarrow is a proven styptic. As a poultice, for example, fresh yarrow can stop bleeding from a cut in minutes.

Similar relieving effects have also been observed with sprains and pulls. Applying a poultice of yarrow and elder can reduce both pain and swelling in something like a twisted ankle. And as it heals cuts and other injuries, yarrow also acts as a strong bacteria killer, especially valuable in a medical climate where more and more germs are becoming resistant to the antibiotics western medicine has come to rely on. Yarrow will even induce sweating as it cleanses the body, helping it escape from the throes of fever.

**Homer credits Achilles with being the first person to use yarrow's healing properties.**

Topix Media Lab
For inquiries, call 646-838-6637

Copyright 2019 Topix Media Lab

Published by Topix Media Lab
14 Wall Street, Suite 4B
New York, NY 10005

Printed in the U.S.

All rights reserved. No part of this publication may be reproduced in any form or by any electronic or mechanical means, including information storage and retrieval systems, without permission in writing from the publisher, except by a reviewer, who may quote brief passages in a review.

Certain photographs used in this publication are used by license or permission from the owner thereof, or are otherwise publicly available. This publication is not endorsed by any person or entity appearing herein. Any product names, logos, brands or trademarks featured or referred to in the publication are the property of their respective trademark owners. Topix Media Lab is not affiliated with, nor sponsored or endorsed by, any of the persons, entities, product names, logos, brands or other trademarks featured or referred to in any of its publications.

**Note to our readers**
The information in this publication has been carefully researched, and every reasonable effort has been made to ensure its accuracy. Neither the publication's publisher nor its creators assume any responsibility for any accidents, injuries, losses or other damages that might come from its use. You are solely responsible for taking any and all reasonable and necessary precautions when performing the activities detailed in its pages.

The information in this publication should not be substituted for, or used to alter, medical therapy without your doctor's advice. For a specific health problem, consult your physician for guidance.

ISBN: 978-1-948174-55-8

**CEO** Tony Romando

**Vice President & Publisher** Phil Sexton
**Senior Vice President of Sales & New Markets** Tom Mifsud
**Vice President of Retail Sales & Logistics** Linda Greenblatt
**Director of Finance** Vandana Patel
**Manufacturing Director** Nancy Puskuldjian
**Financial Analyst** Matthew Quinn
**Brand Marketing & Promotions Assistant** Emily McBride

**Editor-in-Chief** Jeff Ashworth
**Creative Director** Steven Charny
**Photo Director** Dave Weiss
**Managing Editor** Courtney Kerrigan
**Senior Editor** Tim Baker

**Content Editor** Juliana Sharaf
**Art Director** Susan Dazzo
**Associate Photo Editor** Catherine Armanasco
**Associate Editor** Trevor Courneen
**Copy Editor & Fact Checker** Benjamin VanHoose

**Co-Founders** Bob Lee, Tony Romando

All photos Shutterstock except:
p9 Courtesy University of Hawaii/Wikimedia Commons;
p93 uwdigitalcollections/Wikimedia Commons.

CPSIA information can be obtained
at www.ICGtesting.com
Printed in the USA
JSHW012006170621
16011JS00001B/1